HIDDEN FILES

Law Enforcement's True Case Stories of the Unexplained and Paranormal

Sue Kovach

CONTEMPORARY BOOKS

Library of Congress Cataloging-in-Publication Data

Kovach, Sue.
     Hidden files: law enforcement's true case stories of the unexplained
and paranormal / Sue Kovach.
          p.   cm.
     ISBN 0-8092-3121-2
     1. Parapsychology—Case studies.   2. Occultism—Case studies.
3. Police—Miscellanea.   I. Title.
BF1040.K68   1997
133′ .0973—dc21   97-18251
                                                                  CIP

Excerpt from "Pioneers" by J. E. McTeer from *Fifty Years as a Low Country Witch
Doctor,* copyright © 1976 by J. E. McTeer. Reprinted by permission.

Cover photograph copyright © Andy Caulfield/The Image Bank
Cover design by Todd Petersen
Interior design by Scott Rattray

Published by Contemporary Books
An imprint of NTC/Contemporary Publishing Company
4255 West Touhy Avenue, Lincolnwood (Chicago), Illinois 60646 -1975 U.S.A.
Copyright © 1998 by Sue Kovach
Printed in the United States of America
International Standard Book Number: 0-8092-3121-2

15   14   13   12   11   10   9   8   7   6   5   4   3   2   1

To my mother, Judy — the apple never falls far from the tree.

CONTENTS

ACKNOWLEDGMENTS

I AM GRATEFUL to the many people who played an important part in this work, from concept to reality.

Many thanks to my editor, Linda Gray, and project editor, Gerilee Hundt, for their enthusiasm and support, and to the rest of the staff of Contemporary Books.

Thank you to David Vigliano, my agent.

I wish to acknowledge the following people for their contributions: Constable Grant Fredericks of the Vancouver Police Department, Inspector John Grant of the Royal Canadian Mounted Police, and Captain Thomas Yazzie of the Navajo Nation Division of Public Safety, Department of Criminal Investigations, for their assistance and information; Muriel MacFarlane and Martha Moffett for invaluable research guidance and Paulette Cooper for her savvy advice; Jean Brown, Assistant State Section Director, Tampa Bay Mutual UFO Network (MUFON) and UFO researcher Stan Gordon for their assistance; photo guru Ray Fairall; the authors of the Illinois Freedom of Information Act; and Bill Brann, Noah Lukeman, and John Blosser.

My gratitude to the following journalists for their time and assistance: Ron Colquitt (*Mobile Press-Register*); Brian Coxford (BCTV Channel 11, Vancouver, British Columbia); Zack Van Eyke (*Deseret News*, Salt Lake City); Adam Lisberg (*Southtown*

News, Chicago); Debbie Radick (*Beaufort Gazette*, Beaufort, South Carolina); Robert Sands (*Southshore Press*, Long Island, New York); Wes Smith (*Chicago Tribune*); and Barbara McLintock (*The Province,* Vancouver, British Columbia).

A special thank you to Bob Smith and Maggie Morris for the hours they spent proofreading the manuscript and for their thoughtful comments and suggestions.

Warm personal thanks to Lorraine Zenka, Peggy Riglin, and Gilda Carle for all their encouragement and support that helped bring this book about; and to my family, friends, and colleagues for their good wishes.

Introduction

LAW ENFORCEMENT OFFICERS sometimes encounter exceptional situations, marked by strange or unexplainable circumstances: a brush with the occult, perhaps; an encounter with psychic phenomena; an outré sighting; or mysterious events that simply can't be explained by any laws of science we know. Whether these encounters with the unknown occur on or off the job, they leave unanswered questions that may linger for years.

Hidden Files is a collection of true stories of the unexplained from law enforcement officers across the United States and Canada, stories that range from the baffling to the truly bizarre. Most incidents involve actual police cases and occurred while the officer was on duty; a few entail personal experiences. But all are thought-provoking and provide a look at unexplained phenomena from a decidedly different perspective.

Why talk to police about the unexplained? It's not that cops get called out to investigate a haunted house every day, but once in a while it happens. In recent years, police are more likely to encounter psychic phenomena, as more law enforcement departments are accepting assistance from psychics in their investigation of high-profile cases. This is particularly true of missing persons cases, which can have circumstances as eerie as any paranormal occurrence. According to experts, cult and occult activities are on the rise, and police are right in the middle of it all. I personally wanted to hear the first-hand experiences of police officers who have encountered such phenomena because, for one thing, cops are regarded as highly credible witnesses.

For example, the U.S. government considers police officers to be among the most believable witnesses to UFO events; as trained observers, cops notice events going on around them in great detail. They are also trained to be analytical thinkers and puzzle solvers who work daily with hard facts, whose job it is to solve mysteries by considering everything and anything, no matter how improbable the "clues" may be. For those of us who have a fascination with the unexplained—and especially for those who continually question such phenomena—these eyewitness accounts offer a higher-than-average amount of credibility.

Paradoxically (but perhaps understandably), police officers rarely discuss their own encounters with "civilians," or even members of their own profession, for fear of their professional credibility coming into question; therefore, I expected that my search for cops who were willing to talk about their paranormal experiences for this book would be a difficult one. But generally I found that wasn't the case. I was amazed at how many remarkable stories police officers had to tell and surprised at how candid they were willing to be. Once I had gained their trust, most spoke openly, no matter how fantastic the subject was. But a few did need some persuasion, and there were some that no amount of persuasion would convince, who for different reasons did not want to talk about their experiences.

The blunt truth is that for cops there's little to gain and possibly much to lose from talking openly about their encounters with the paranormal. Even though the incidents were very real, some officers didn't want to open themselves to ridicule—or worse. And their fears aren't unfounded. One officer believes his openness about a UFO encounter cost him his job; another remained quiet for 20 years about his encounter with an unknown creature because of the derision he suffered from talking about it at the time. Another officer who had had a similar experience wrestled with the idea of telling me about it, but finally confided to a close friend that he just wanted to put the 15-year-old event behind him. Obviously, he still hadn't accomplished that goal.

Cops are often placed in positions where they may be likely to encounter a lot of weird things. Chief Douglas Glamann of the Horicon Police Department in Wisconsin related how, as a young patrol officer sitting in a squad car on the graveyard shift, he and his partner would sometimes see mysterious, unexplained lights "bouncing across the sky." On one such night, as the pair watched the weird lights, they kept glancing nervously at the radio mike hanging on the console between them. Their conversation went something like this:

"You call it in."

"Uh-uh . . . *you* call it in."

"*I'm* not gonna call it in. *You* call it in!"

It's no surprise that it never got called in. But today, Chief Glamann is more willing to discuss such strange events because of a bizarre case of poltergeist activity that occurred in his town in 1988. The case threw both him and his community into the media spotlight, forcing him to take a stand on the issue in full public view. Glamann addresses the case later in this book.

Despite the increased popularity of the study of paranormal phenomena, there is still a paranoia associated with discussing them. I think it's unnecessary. What appears to be magic, supernatural, or out of this world could have rational, even scientific explanations we have yet to discover. *Paranormal* literally means "beyond normal"—but normal is relative. In ancient times, people thought an eclipse of the sun was caused by a huge cosmic animal taking a bite out of it. They greatly feared the event and believed the end of the world was upon them. They tried to explain an eclipse in terms of what they knew, and at that time they knew of little beyond their own small plots of land. The answer was there, but they weren't capable of finding it nor comprehending it.

We know today what an eclipse is, of course, but we may not be advanced enough to understand what we now call paranormal. Someday, after further study and research, we may also have solid explanations for these phenomena. For that reason, I think *unexplained* is a better word to use than *paranormal*, because it just means that all the facts aren't in. Kevin Humphreys, a forensic investigator for a police agency in Oregon, agrees that we need to get the facts and believes that scientific study will eventually explain the unexplained.

"You can't have a closed mind. A closed mind can close out the truth, and today's fictions may be tomorrow's truths," says Humphreys. "We need scientific explanations for these things. I say let's research them and discover the explanations. Right now all we can do is put together as many pieces of the puzzle as we can. Based on that work, we can make determinations with a certain scientific degree of certainty about what is most likely going on."

But no one can be completely certain about unexplained phenomena if little or no physical evidence exists. Until such evidence is found, we must rely on eyewitness accounts to determine for ourselves what to believe. After hearing some of the police officers' stories contained in this book, my own thinking about certain phenomena changed considerably.

The purpose of *Hidden Files* is to present law enforcement officers' encounters with the unexplained for the reader's consideration. Each incident is told in story format, based on extensive interviews with the police officers involved and on information obtained from public records. No attempt is made to prove or disprove the events. Each chapter covers a specific topic, with background material and discussion from experts to help shed some light on the officers' experiences. This information is something to keep in mind as you explore each story and try to draw conclusions of your own.

All the police officers interviewed for this book spoke on

the record for the express purpose of having their stories included. In some cases, I used fictitious names for witnesses or participants other than police officers. For example, certain psychics who work with police did not want publicity. In other cases, the circumstances surrounding certain events dictated the use of fictitious names. These names are indicated with an asterisk (*) at first use.

One constant theme throughout the book is the remarkable open-mindedness of the officers involved. No matter how unusual, frightening, or wonderful their experiences, each officer was willing to consider the possibility that, for some things, there are no pat answers. I'm sure that readers who are fascinated with tales of the unexplained will find their own beliefs and ideas challenged by these stories as much as I did.

1

GHOSTS

PEOPLE BELIEVE IN GHOSTS. Really, they do. Just watch the look on their faces anytime someone suggests a ghost might be present. Their eyes get wide, they glance quickly over each shoulder, and then they laugh and say, "Yeah, sure." But remember, their first reaction is the authentic one.

Perhaps people aren't certain *what* they think about ghosts and spirits. Even if you believe in the concept of life after death, it can be difficult to accept the idea of disembodied beings unless you've seen or experienced one. It appears, however, that many people have. Stories abound throughout history of ghosts that have appeared to haunt the living; of spirits who intervene in worldly events to prevent harm to people; of those who simply wander the Earth with no clear purpose or intent. Some are even said to be malevolent, though most parapsychologists believe ghosts are more often benign and even helpful. One thing is certain: Ghost stories are enduring and can be found as far back as the beginning of recorded history.

What exactly are ghosts and spirits? According to Loyd Auerbach, director of the Office of Paranormal Investigations (OPI) in Orinda, California, and author of the book *ESP, Hauntings and Poltergeists*, two different experiences make up the phenomenon: apparitions and hauntings.

"An apparition is everyone's traditional idea of a ghost. A person's consciousness or personality somehow manages to survive the death of the body, and that spirit can remain in a specific location," says Auerbach. "It shows intelligence and consciousness, and it often interacts with people on a recurring basis."

It's possible to experience a ghost without even realizing it, because sometimes a spirit will manifest as a rush of air or simply a strong presence. Interaction can occur in several different ways, including sight, sound, touch, and even smell. Some of the best ghost stories of the American South involve the sweet aroma of magnolia blossoms.

A haunting, however, is a noninteractive encounter. According to Auerbach, most reported cases of ghostly activities tend to be hauntings unless they happen within 48 hours of the spirit's worldly death. Hauntings occur in a specific location, can last for centuries, and are not believed to involve ghosts in the traditional sense. They are more of an imprint on the environment, the mark of a person or event that happened as little as five years ago or as far back as 500 years ago. Under certain conditions, the imprint can be detected by the living.

"Whenever you have figures or sounds locked in a pattern that repeats over and over again, that's a haunting," Auerbach says. "It's actually fairly common."

Most people would have little trouble noticing a haunting, which can manifest as rattling windows, slamming doors, and other physical episodes. But even the nonphysical aspects of a haunting—such as the strong sense of a presence nearby—might be felt because we all have the ability to pick up these environmental impressions. We do it on a daily basis.

"Walk into a place you've never been before, and you'll notice that it either feels good or it feels bad—and generally, your feelings prove out," Auerbach says. "Visit some friends and see what you feel. If it's negative, did the couple have a fight the night before? You're probably picking that up." People tend, however, to discount such feelings, or we're so used to them that we don't think about what the feelings actually mean.

Still, not everyone can see ghosts even if they want to. Auerbach investigates ghosts all the time, but he has yet to actually see one, and he must communicate with ghosts through a person who can see them. Certainly he believes in ghosts, but he says belief has little or nothing to do with being able to see them. Auerbach regards ghosts as a mental phenomenon, not a physically visual one. He believes that what people see is literally a hallucination—but one with an outside cause.

"One part of perception is eyes and ears, and the second part is mental processing," he says. "What your eyes see is not the whole picture. The brain interprets visual information and will add to or subtract from it depending on what's going on."

Could this explain why people usually see ghosts wearing clothing? We can assume no department stores exist in ghostly dimensions. Because clothing itself wasn't alive at one time, as the spectre inhabiting the clothes was, where does the image of it come from? Auerbach once asked a spirit to explain.

"The ghost said that she's actually a ball of energy, but she still thought of herself the way she looked when she was alive," he says. "People who were sensitive enough to see her picked up her self-image, and she saw herself wearing clothing. If she had always worn a favorite perfume while alive, they might have actually smelled it."

Proving that ghosts exist is even more difficult if ghosts can be seen only by some people and not others. Physically it's an impossibility, and for a very good reason. By definition, a ghost is a disembodied consciousness or mind. As yet we have no physical evidence for the existence of the human mind or consciousness *in* the body, let alone *out* of it. Rather, we infer it by observation. With ghosts, we can come closest to proving their existence by gathering anecdotal information from witnesses and obtaining specific details about the ghost's life when he or she was alive. This information can then be researched. If the characteristics the spirit displays can be matched to those of the ghost when he or she was alive, and if information the spirit has relayed can be verified (particularly if the information is specific and not likely to be known by others), the existence of the apparition can be proved, to a greater or lesser degree.

"We'd have less trouble proving in court that ghosts exist than we would in a scientific arena," says Auerbach. "Witnesses who say ghosts don't exist didn't see anything; witnesses who say they *do* exist *did* see something. If the information they got from the ghost jibes with what can be proven about the ghost before it died—and if there was no other way to have known that information beforehand—a court would likely rule that the ghost exists."

So if conscious minds do indeed wander around after the body dies, why do they do it? Because they don't know they're dead, says Auerbach. They continue to act like living beings because they are denying their own death.

Auerbach has investigated a case involving a ghost who actually argued about its state of being with the people living in its former residence.

"Get out of my house!" said the ghost.

"It's not your house anymore. You're dead," the family replied.

"No, I'm *not*! Get out of my house!"

Based on years of research, Auerbach is convinced that another reason ghosts linger is because they want company. Therefore, the last place you should ever expect to find one is in a cemetery. Why would they want to hang around in a place where there are no living people?

"The ghost's behavior is much the same as when it was alive, and people tend to want to be around people," he says. "That's why places like restaurants often have ghosts—they simply go back to their old hangouts."

People who do encounter ghosts and want to know more about them sometimes contact the Office of Paranormal Investigations for information or suggestions on how to deal with a ghostly situation. On occasion, the calls come from police officers.

Cops and Ghosts

Although it's rare for OPI to hear from law enforcement about apparitions, they do get a few calls a year, says Auerbach. Situations where police need information in this area may not happen that often—or perhaps the cops just don't ask. Most often, a police officer will call because he or she was sent on a case where a citizen had ghostly activity in the home and the officer was personally interested in investigating the situation more closely. But officially police don't bother with ghost cases unless a crime may be involved.

One example is in the town of Greenburg, New York. Every year, particularly around Halloween, police get reports that people have seen the ghost of the Headless Horseman at Sleepy Hollow Cemetery. Auerbach says in 1978 there were reports of people who vanished in that area. But he doesn't know just how seriously police took the reports. "That is Washington Irving territory, and it has a lot of mystique around it. His house is supposedly haunted."

Another example is in a suburb of Dallas, Texas, where police have checked on possible break-ins at a popular restaurant that is alleged to be haunted. Locals say figures could be seen moving around inside the building after closing time. When police looked through the windows, they reportedly saw a woman in flowing white attire who vanished right before their eyes.

If police do want to know how they should go about investigating a ghost report, Auerbach explains to them how he conducts his own investigations. He tells police not to automatically assume that anyone making a report is crazy just because the person says he or she is seeing a ghost. It could be a pillar of the community having the experience, and the person may be mistaking a normal occurrence for something paranormal. So police should look for worldly explanations first.

"I ask lots of questions and see how the story holds together," he says. "I'll ask what makes the people think there's a ghost in the house—if they say noises, I'll check to see if the house is settling or there's a squirrel in the attic. I also look around to get a handle on how the people spend their time and ask if they've seen any scary movies lately or read any scary books. Something like that could cause them to miss the obvious explanations."

If a concrete explanation can't be found, the next step is to address the question of mental stability. If the person making the report can see the ghost, Auerbach has him or her ask the ghost what it wants and suggest that the situation can be resolved if everyone cooperates. The information gleaned in this way can be quite telling.

"Depending on what I'm told after the person questions the ghost, it will be very obvious if that person has a psychological problem or if he's getting some genuine information," Auerbach says. "For example, if the ghost is supposedly making typical ghost noises, saying 'boo' or bringing a message of the end of the world, I figure I've probably got a person with a psychological problem. Also, getting into mundane, down-to-earth details will tip the hand, because a psychologically unstable person will miss those details."

If the ghost says its privacy is being invaded and it doesn't like the intrusion, that's a more real, down-to-earth circumstance. Auerbach then handles the encounter as a basic crisis intervention situation that requires talking things over with both sides. Police may find it helpful to get the homeowners involved in the process by encouraging them to try verifying any factual information the ghost may provide. "I can say, 'Hey, you've got all this information now, aren't you the least bit curious to find out if it's true?' I can suggest they go to county records to check it out," he says. "People who thought the ghost was going to kill them can now learn all about who it was. It relieves the fear."

It also provides an opportunity to get rid of the ghost. Once the people know what the spirit wants and what's bothering it, the situation might be resolved.

Police have had some great—and some not-so-great—ghost encounters. Most were positive experiences, as you'll see in the following true stories. In *"U'hane"* (the Hawaiian word for "spirit"), we meet Detective Lieutenant Jim Duff of Honolulu, who investigated a ghost report and discovered something that the police had long been looking for. In "The Shaman of Teslin Lake," the spirit of a native medicine man intervened to save the life of a Royal Canadian Mounted Police constable in 1986, and the magic of that moment continues today in some very real, down-to-earth ways. In northern California, a sheriff's deputy searching for two missing people follows the lead of an apparition sighting to a conclusion that is both tragic and triumphant. Finally, in West Virginia, state police troopers relate some odd experiences at one of their installations in "The Barracks."

U'hane

Detective Lieutenant Jim Duff (retired)
(COURTESY OF JIM DUFF)

In Hawaii, you don't carry raw pork in your car when you're driving over the Pali Highway on Oahu. If you do, the car will surely break down, and you'll be stranded. Or you might glance in the rearview mirror and be startled to see an old woman sitting in the back seat, a strange apparition that will vanish if you turn your head to look. It's unclear exactly why raw pork will cause such anomalies, but why take chances? In that area along Route 61, which crosses the Koolau Mountain Range between Honolulu and Kaneohe, the warriors of King Kamehameha I destroyed the armies of Oahu by pushing them over a cliff in the early 1800s, thus uniting all of the islands. It is an area filled with mysticism, as are most of the Hawaiian Islands, America's paradise on earth, a land with a culture rich in folklore and superstition. It makes an interesting beat for a cop, who can bump into islanders' beliefs fairly often. Many police officers ignore any references to such folklore, brushing them off with a snicker. But there are many others who, while not adherents themselves, don't discount these beliefs or, more important, the people who hold them.

Honolulu Police Department homicide detective Jim Duff is one of those cops.

Detective Duff was fully prepared for some ribbing once he got over his surprise at the contents of a hand-scrawled note his lieutenant handed him one day in 1986. The note said, in effect, "See a woman about a ghost." The lieutenant grinned broadly.

"Have *I* got a case for *you*," he sang.

"Like what?" Duff asked impatiently.

"The people at this clothing factory say a ghost has appeared over there," the lieutenant replied. "Now it may or may not have something to do with this unsolved homicide case." He was still grinning as he dropped a file in front of Duff. "Of course, we'd like you to check it out."

Of course, thought Duff. I'm junior man on the squad and this is what I'm going to get. The case in front of him was familiar, though he had not been working homicide when it had happened. The body of Kimo Apana* had been found in a parked car in a lot near Honolulu International Airport more than a year before. The man had been beaten severely and strangled. Investigators determined that the parking lot was not the scene of the murder. But the few leads they had had dried up fast, and no others had been found. The case was put in the pending files.

As luck or fate would have it, the current ghost-sighting reports were coming from a clothing factory once owned by Apana's wife, Leilani*, who had briefly been considered a suspect in the case. The connection caught Duff's attention.

"I may not believe in paranormal things, and I may not believe in a lot of the Hawaiian superstitions, but I knew I had to look into it," says Duff, recently retired from the force. "If the people there believed they had seen a ghost, then that belief must have had a pretty strong basis in something. I couldn't just discount the reports out of hand."

Leilani Apana had sold the factory shortly after her husband's death. The new owner graciously allowed Duff and his partner free access to look around and to question the employees who had reported the ghost. At first, the seamstresses were hesitant to talk about their experience, especially in front of their coworkers. But the detectives pulled the women aside for personal interviews and soon got a picture of what was going on. One particular area of the shop, located at the base of a staircase leading to the owner's quarters upstairs, seemed to be the center of the ghostly activity. The women explained it was more of a presence than an actual sighting. Several of them confessed to having felt a cold chill at the base of the stairs and said they could sense "him" in the room. Duff asked who "he" was.

Kimo Apana, they replied. The employees all knew Kimo because he used to come to the factory quite often when his wife owned it. Now they could feel him brush past them and, from time to time, feel a rush of icy cold air. At the same time they always noticed a distinctive aroma: the pleasant fragrance of the particular pomade, or hair-styling grease, that Kimo used to slick back his ample mane. The women all felt uneasy at these sensations and were certain that Kimo was haunting their work area.

Duff didn't want to ignore what they were saying, especially since the factory had not been checked out before. Leilani hadn't allowed it. Though some felt she was a good suspect from the start, police had had no evidence and no motive to push for warrants to search the facility. Duff now had a chance to take a look, armed with a new investigative tool.

"We had this new scientific process for locating blood,

using a chemical called Luminol that would glow in the dark when it came into contact with the substance. I thought I'd try it out," says Duff. "We came back that night after the shop was closed and all the employees had gone."

The first site the team checked was the owner's quarters upstairs. If there had been a murder at the factory, this seemed the most likely spot. The Luminol showed nothing. Duff next theorized that the body may have been dragged down the stairs, so the staircase was sprayed with the chemical. Again, no results.

Finally, he decided to check the area at the bottom of the stairs, the spot where the workers had sensed Kimo's ghost.

Duff doused the area with the chemical. The concrete floor lit up with speckles of fluorescent blue light in swirl patterns, the kind a mop would make when used to clean up blood. With chills scooting up and down his spine, Duff now felt the ghost reports were indeed significant to this case. The only spot out of three where blood showed up was the same place the ghost had been sensed. The spooky Luminol glow traced a path to a drainpipe in the floor. Who could know how many times that floor had been washed, Duff marveled, and still the blood made its mark. He considered digging up the floor and the drainpipe, despite the considerable destruction that would make, in hopes of finding a larger quantity of blood.

But more Luminol spraying showed another path of trace blood, one that led to the opposite wall. Here, the base of the wall glowed brightly. It was quite possible the killer had tried to hose down the floor, sending streams of water and blood splashing against the wall. The liquid then might have seeped underneath and become trapped. But this portion of wall was a big, thick piece of very new plywood board. The shop's current owner had been nice to let them in, and Duff didn't want to start cutting up her walls on what might amount to a wild-goose chase at this point. Yes, he had a Luminol hit, but that was *all* he had—a hit that showed trace amounts, not even enough to collect a decent sample. It was a solid lead, but nothing much beyond that.

In Honolulu, using single-wall construction to divide rooms is very common. This practice makes it difficult for the islands' termite population to find good hiding places, thus saving home and business owners a lot of money and aggravation. Directly on the other side of this particular wall was another clothing factory. The owners were present at the time and allowed the detectives to inspect their side of the wall in question. Duff was surprised to find it covered with a lightweight veneer paneling that made a double wall no one would have guessed existed. The owners agreed to let the detectives remove the paneling, which came off easily. As if to prove the rationale for single walls, the two-by-fours in this spot were pithy and termite-eaten. Crime scene technicians lifted the fragmented board from the flooring and made a startling discovery: under the board was a substantial amount of a caked-up substance that closely resembled dried blood.

"You have to be analytical about it and say that it *looked* like blood. Maybe it was and maybe it wasn't. The technician was able to scrape up three vials," says Duff. Luminol was sprayed in the area, and the results elicited a whoop of delight from the team. "The whole thing lit up. You could have read a book or a newspaper by it—it glowed so brightly that it threw shadows," Duff recalls. "That was *very* spooky, but to us it was as good as seeing Hank Aaron hit a home run."

Naturally, Duff's superior was dumbfounded, as was the whole homicide unit. Even Duff's partner, who had been humoring him all along, had to admit that seriously checking out the ghost lead had been the right thing to do. As far as Duff was concerned, he had found the place where the murder had been committed, and the evidence pointed straight at the widow Leilani.

But more proof was needed. Luckily, police still had a sample of Kimo's blood on file, so another new technology was called into play. That sample and the floor scrapings were sent to a lab for DNA testing. On the day of Duff's fortieth birthday, he got the call telling him the match was 99.999 percent.

This was the first successful use of DNA testing in Honolulu. Duff's investigative group was suddenly on the cutting edge.

Now there was sufficient cause to look closely at the Apanas' life together. "I found out that the relationship had not been good and that, interestingly, there had been quite a lot of insurance taken out on the victim's life. Some of it—in fact, most of it—the victim never knew about," Duff says. "There was fraud involved and there was forgery involved. We were able to prove with handwriting analysis that Kimo's signatures on the policy documents had been forged. Further, there was only one primary beneficiary of all the policies: Leilani."

Adding insult to possible murder, Duff discovered that Leilani had bounced the check for the premium. Three weeks after the insurance policies finally went into effect, Kimo was killed.

"That bounced check—I kept thinking it might actually have extended his life a bit," says Duff. Why hadn't anyone discovered the large amount of life insurance before? "I don't know. You had the bereaved widow, the kids who were all torn up about it, and a simple working couple. These were not huge corporate executives, wealthy people, or movie stars. On the surface, everything seemed on the up-and-up; but if you thought about white-collar crime at all and really dug in, it was like Pandora's box."

A quick look at the business insurance policies revealed that the factory had a sophisticated burglar alarm system, one that employed an internal microphone for monitoring. In what few would call a coincidence, the alarm system was working perfectly except for the night of Kimo's murder. According to the monitoring company's records, the routine phone call from Leilani to turn on the system was never made. The system wasn't activated again until the next night. Based on these facts and the forensic evidence, Leilani Apana was arrested for the murder of her husband.

But Duff and his team were to learn that the cutting edge can be a lonely place. The case made it to the preliminary hearing stage, but no further. A few motions to recover some items of evidence were heard by the state supreme court, and the district attorney wanted additional follow-up on the case. But by then Duff had transferred out of homicide. Eventually, the file ended up in somebody else's desk drawer, where it sits today. "To sum it up," Duff says slowly, "they felt there wasn't a sufficient amount of blood located at the factory to say that, in fact, Kimo Apana was killed there." So why was his blood all over the floor? "Well, maybe he cut himself," Duff says sarcastically. He pauses. "Maybe the science in this case was too new and not well understood by those involved. I only wish I could have brought the suspect to justice."

Duff feels that while he's not necessarily more of a believer in such paranormal occurrences, he's perhaps less skeptical. He's never seen a ghost himself and never had a conversation with one. Most of what he deals with on a daily basis has a tangible explanation. But he admits there are some situations that cannot be explained, including the case of Kimo Apana.

"Maybe now I'll be the first to come out and tell people you don't *ever* discount anything until you can prove it solid. Don't knock it until you've looked into it."

And what of the chilling, unseen spirit of Kimo Apana? He hasn't been observed since then, so apparently he accomplished what he wanted or needed to accomplish—to have the truth revealed. Kimo must have felt it was enough that Jim Duff believed him, even if he didn't exactly believe *in* him.

When visiting Hawaii, it's best to pay attention to what the locals have to say, and Duff offers one piece of advice: don't you dare take home any of those lava rocks strewn around the island's volcanoes. Madam Pele, the fire goddess who makes the volcanoes erupt, is a bit touchy about such things. *Mahalo.*

The Shaman of Teslin Lake

It was a day much like that fateful day in March 1985: the sun struggled to peek through gray clouds that cast a gloom over frozen Teslin Lake in northern British Columbia, Canada. Deep snow blanketed the ground and bitter cold iced the air.

On this day, March 19, 1995, a small group of people journeyed to the remote location to commemorate the 10-year anniversary of a tragic event: the murder of Royal Canadian Mounted Police (RCMP) Constable Mike Buday. A TV reporter said it was spooky, because incredibly, just like that day 10 years ago, a lone bald eagle circled overhead. In the distance, a flock of trumpeter swans glided by in straight-line formation, their presence unusual for March in the far north.

Ten years before, an RCMP Emergency Response Team had arrived at the British Columbia–Yukon border to apprehend fugitive Michael Oros for the murder of a trapper. During the encounter, Constable Mike Buday was shot by Oros, who in turn was killed by Constable Garry Rodgers in what is still said to be a completely impossible shot. The facts surrounding the death of Constable Buday are well documented. But few know what local Tlingits, the aboriginal people, think happened that day—that a spiritual intervention saved the life of Garry Rodgers. The bullet that killed Michael Oros was guided by the spirit of a dead shaman angered by Oros the night before the shootings.

Michael Oros was the stuff of legend—an American draft dodger who'd fled from Kansas to the wilds of northern Canada during the early 1970s. He lived alone in the remote, isolated bush. In this area where inhabitants can live without human contact for months at a time, the already disturbed Oros slowly lost his mind and became as untamed as his surroundings. Oros terrorized the vast wilderness for 13 years, stealing from other trappers and totally disregarding all laws. He soon earned himself the nickname "Mad Trapper of Teslin Lake."

Diaries found in Oros's various cabins and on his person contained bizarre entries that revealed an extremely paranoid individual, one who no longer distinguished his dreams from reality. He believed that authorities were secretly spraying him with mind-altering drugs. Oros wrote: "I will kill them, my bullet wants to eat pork." He also expressed hatred for "the horrible straight people," whom he believed were out to corner him. Even more disturbing, the diaries also revealed Oros's admiration for another notorious legend, Albert Johnson, who was immortalized on film in a Charles Bronson movie, *Death Hunt* (1981). Johnson, the, "Mad Trapper of Rat River," murdered two mounties and spurred a massive manhunt throughout the Yukon in the 1930s. Oros felt a strong kinship with the killer Johnson and, purposefully or not, began to emulate him.

Oros achieved most-wanted status after he murdered another trapper and then ransacked a cabin along the lake. Tracking and capturing him would not be an easy task. Oros was a skilled backwoodsman who trapped, hunted, and lived off the land. He knew his way around the bush, and over time had learned how to blend into it. The RCMP sent a crack team after him, one specially trained for this type of wilderness mission. To get to the remote area and find Oros, police had to fly in by helicopter. None of the officers involved believed for a moment that Oros would give up without a fight. To make matters worse, he knew the manhunt was on. But the highly skilled RCMP team members were confident in themselves and their training.

Says Garry Rodgers, Constable Mike Buday's partner and best friend, "I felt that Mike was next to invincible. He was tremendously powerful; he had exceptionally good eyesight, hearing, and common sense; and his shooting ability was phenomenal. You couldn't want a better guy to be looking after you."

The RCMP team landed near the lake, then assembled their gear and set off. Clad in white camouflage fatigues and snowshoes, the team split into two groups—three men moved off to the north, while Rodgers, Buday, and another officer went to the south. Oros was caught between them, or so they thought. Despite being outgunned six to one, the Mad Trapper managed to turn the tables on the mounties. At first, he went on the defensive, entering the thick trees at Teslin Lake's edge. While the mounties lay in wait by the lake, expecting to see Oros emerge from the woods, the Mad Trapper out-maneuvered them.

"Oros was behind us within 10 minutes. It was perfectly planned out—he knew exactly what he was doing," says Rodgers.

Through waist-deep snow, the Mad Trapper had circled behind the mounties as stealthily as if he were tracking a moose. He got to within 50 feet of Buday and his dog, Trooper, without ever alerting them. Oros then positioned himself so that he had a clear shot at Buday and Rodgers without moving from his snowshoes or losing his balance.

Recalls Rodgers: "I'm looking around, just watching, and out of the corner of my eye I caught what I thought was a movement. I looked through a small gap in the trees, and I could see what I thought was the shape of a face. And as I put my eyes onto it, it almost illuminated like a lightbulb. I knew it was Oros, and I either radioed or yelled to Mike, 'He's right behind you!' As soon as I said that, there was a shot fired."

That shot from Oros's rifle killed Buday instantly.

"I couldn't see the rifle; I couldn't see his hands. All I could

Garry Rodgers points out the scene to Staff Sergeant Ed Hill (L) and artist Roy Vickers. (COURTESY OF B. MCLINTOCK)

Constable Garry Rodgers displays a picture of Constable Mike Buday and dog Trooper. (COURTESY OF B. MCLINTOCK)

sec was his head," Rodgers continues. "I could sense the shape and the movement of him working the rifle's bolt back, closing it, turning over, and pointing right at me. Instinctively, I turned and fired the gun, and by the time I recovered from the shot, the face was gone—just disappeared."

With a pivot and one quick shot, with no time to aim through the dense brush and thick tree trunks, Rodgers had dropped Oros in his tracks. But this was no ordinary shot and, as all would soon learn, other mysterious circumstances surrounded the Mad Trapper's death.

When investigators checked the scene afterward, they examined Oros's weapon, a bolt-action 303 British army rifle. They found that after shooting Buday, Oros had ejected a shell casing, put a new round into the rifle, closed the bolt, pointed at Rodgers, and pulled the trigger. Rodgers didn't know at the time that Oros was attempting to shoot him—the rifle had mysteriously misfired before Rodgers got off his killing shot. If the misfire had not happened, Rodgers would certainly have been felled as well.

"Something stopped that round from going off. There was nothing the matter with the firearm, and, presumably, there was nothing wrong with this particular round," says Rodgers, fingering the bullet that should have killed him. "It's exactly the same as the other round. The firing pin punctured it . . . it just didn't go off."

Local Tlingits are certain they know why the round failed. The night before, Oros had slept on Shaman's Island in the middle of Teslin Lake. The island is the burial ground of a shaman, or medicine man, and is considered a sacred place by the Tlingit people. Oros had brought a curse upon himself, they say, by violating the sanctity of that island. The angry spirit of the departed shaman took matters into his own hands. It was the shaman's spirit who caused Oros's gun to misfire and who helped guide Rodgers's bullet on its impossible path through the narrowest of openings in the dense trees.

Still somewhat baffled by his accurate shot, Rodgers agrees. "To duplicate that shot under those conditions, I think, is just about impossible. I've never been able to explain that. I picked up the gun, I pointed the gun, I pulled the trigger— but what guided the bullet is anybody's explanation. Maybe it was a higher power. There was a reason why Mike died; there's a reason why I or any of the other team members weren't killed. I do believe there was an intervention that day."

Ten years later, Rodgers, a few reporters and RCMP chaplain Father Tim Coonan returned to the site in commemoration of the tragedy, accompanied by a prominent native artist Roy Henry Vickers and his fellow artist, RCMP Staff Sergeant Ed Hill. The artists' purpose that day was to gain a vision for a painting to honor Mike Buday. In the native tradition, both artists would search in their own way for the perfect image to capture on canvas. They split up and wandered off. Ed Hill looked to the trees where Buday had died, but no faces appeared, no images became apparent and, most important, he felt no "bristle" within himself. He sat for a while on a point of land, looking at the lake, the island, and the surrounding mountains. For some reason, his mind kept returning to those trees.

"In retrospect, the logical, analytical policeman was awake inside of me, reenacting the events of that day. The policeman *knew* the image must be in the bush," says Hill.

The sun was now out, and he relaxed in its warmth. "I listened for something, waited for something, but the policeman inside me spoke louder than the artist inside me. We'd been there an hour, but I was getting no vision, nothing was coming to me."

Teslin Lake and the mountain Sheep Standing by Himself
(COURTESY OF B. MCLINTOCK)

Hill and Vickers had not really talked much, only smiled at each other when their eyes met. They were searching. Now Hill noticed Vickers walking on the lake, and the policeman quickly left him. He felt the artist stirring inside. He followed Vickers, wondering if it was really going to be this simple. Vickers had stopped, and when Hill stood beside him, the image they had been seeking appeared before them—open water, the mountain, the trees, and the island. It felt perfect. When Hill walked about 10 feet to his right, he lost the image.

Ten feet in the other direction produced the same result. He had to be in that one spot. Hill was bubbling as he described every detail of the future painting. Vickers reflected quietly and smiled, then said, "We've got it!"

Vickers returned to the campsite, but Hill remained on the spot, dropping to his knees in the soft snow, feeling comfortable and peaceful in the perfect place. He soon fell asleep. "I dreamed. I don't remember of what, but they were happy, peaceful, and calm experiences, and then I was awakened abruptly by a raven, which the natives call 'the Trickster,' " says Hill. "I awoke to find my eyes full of tears—I had been crying in my sleep. I turned to watch the raven disappear into the trees, but when I turned back, I was hit hard by what I saw. Now I knew why I had waited in the spot for so long. Before me was a flock of white swans, trumpeter swans, flying right at me." Had he looked a moment earlier or later, he would have missed the image. The swans flew in unison, showing off many varied formations as if posing for him. Hill jumped to his feet, thinking that Vickers hadn't seen the show, but Hill spied him watching the swans from the campsite.

Later that afternoon, Rodgers, Vickers, and Hill sat together on the very spot where Buday had died. While Rodgers recounted the events he had experienced in 1985, they all smoked a ceremonial pipe. As Hill glanced over Vickers's shoulder, he was awestruck by a sudden realization: there in front of him, clearly outlined through the trees, was their vision. The mountain, the island, the open water—it was all there, perfect. In 1985, that view had been Mike Buday's last sight of the world. Hill excitedly told Vickers to turn around. When Vickers saw the image, his smile said, "I told you so!" It was no wonder they had not been permitted to wander a few feet either way on the ice. "We had been at the perfect place at the perfect time," says Hill.

In early June 1995, RCMP and native Canadians gathered for the unveiling of Roy Henry Vickers and Ed Hill's painting.

The painting "Sheep Standing by Himself"
(Reprinted with permission of the artists, Roy H. Vickers and rcmp
Staff Sergeant Ed Hill)

In an attempt to make some good come out of the tragic event, Vickers and Hill are using the proceeds from the painting's sale to fund Vision Quest, a nonprofit program for the long-term treatment of addicted persons from all backgrounds and walks of life. Vickers and Hill's vision in the painting shows an eagle in the clouds spreading its protective wings over the lake and mountain area. Shaman's Island can be seen in the distance. A careful look at the painting reveals the outline of the shaman along the shoreline. The trumpeter swans are there, too, as guardians of the site. It is a true memorial to Mike Buday and to the shaman's spirit—which many people believe saved the life of Garry Rodgers and brought down the notorious Mad Trapper of Teslin Lake.

The Spirit of Motherhood

Deputy Rich Strasser took a particular interest in the missing persons case he was assigned in mid-June 1994: A 24-year-old mother and her 3-year-old son had vanished while driving from the Placerville, California, area to a friend's home in Carson City, Nevada. Christene Skubish and her son Nicky were traveling alone and had taken scenic Highway 50, which runs through El Dorado County to Lake Tahoe. Strasser, himself the father of two young children, was quite concerned about the pair. They had left on June 6, and it was now four days later. Highway 50 was usually congested with Nevada casino-bound traffic, but no one had reported seeing anything related to the disappearance. Nothing, that is, until the early morning hours of Saturday, June 11, when the sighting of what may have been an apparition quickly led Strasser to solve the disappearance. The outcome was both joyous and tragic, marked by strange, unexplained circumstances.

Strasser came on the night shift and began his investigation by talking on the phone with some of the Skubishes' concerned family. They were planning to drive up from southern California to meet with him and to begin their own search. He learned that Christene had left the previous Monday night and had planned to stop for gasoline on the way. The only 24-hour service stations in the area were in Placerville, so Strasser visited each one in hopes of digging up some clues about what may have happened to Christene and Nicky.

At the same time, about 18 miles east of town, Deborah Hoyt and her husband were driving along Route 50, returning to their Lake Tahoe home from a trip. It was 3:00 A.M. and the couple was cruising quietly along a stretch of the highway known locally as Bullion Bend, a name that survived from the old California gold rush days. Suddenly Deborah, in the passenger seat, let out a startled cry. Lying curled up on the shoulder of the road was a naked woman, one arm flung across her face as though to shield it.

"I just started screaming and screaming," said Deborah. Her husband, who hadn't seen the woman, wanted to turn back, but Deborah thought they would do more good by getting to a phone as quickly as possible to call for help. They soon found a forest ranger's station about two miles down the road and called 911. California Highway Patrol officers and sheriff's deputies responded in minutes. The Hoyts immediately led them to the area where Deborah said she'd seen "a naked lady, lying on her side, bent legs together with an arm over her head." But after searching a five-mile stretch of road for nearly an hour, the officers saw no trace of the naked woman—or anything else for that matter. Deborah was insistent that the woman had been there. Unable to do any more, the couple continued on their journey home, still very disturbed by what had happened.

Shortly after 5:00 A.M., Strasser got a call to talk with Deborah Hoyt about her sighting. The investigators on the scene thought the whole scenario was weird and were dismissing it. They did not have the facts regarding the missing persons case. Strasser, on the other hand, didn't take long to put two and two together. He thought the area should be checked again, as the sighting might be connected in some way to the Skubishes' disappearance. Besides, Deborah Hoyt's physical description of the naked woman seemed to match Christene Skubish's appearance.

"I had to go take a look. Deborah Hoyt knew what she saw and was certain that it was not a mistake. The other officers said she had been very adamant about it and wouldn't budge. I theorized there may have been an accident and the woman—possibly Christene Skubish—had been injured," Strasser recalls.

The deputy headed for Bullion Bend. Dawn was just breaking and the deserted roadway looked eerie in the half-light. Strasser slowed his car and drove carefully along the shoulder, searching for any sign of the woman. Then, he spotted a tiny object lying about two feet into the road. In the dim light, he saw it was a shoe. Strasser stopped and picked it up—a toddler's shoe. Puzzled, he walked to the side of the road, where the shoulder quickly dropped off in a steep embankment. It wasn't the kind of slope a person could just walk up or down.

Deputy Rich Strasser, El Dorado County Sheriff's Office (MOUNTAIN DEMOCRAT)

"You would have had to almost climb hand over hand to come up, and getting down safely would best be accomplished by sitting and sliding down the hill on your butt," he says.

Standing at the top of the embankment, Strasser scanned the trees below. Then he saw it. The car was barely visible but had obviously been badly damaged. He could see that part of the roof had been peeled off. The license plate proved it was Christene Skubish's car. Strasser felt a rush of adrenaline and scrambled down the steep embankment, stumbling and falling in his haste to get to the car. He hoped that he'd find the car empty, that Christene and her child had somehow gotten out and were safe. But his hopes were dashed when he neared the vehicle and saw Christene Skubish in the driver's seat, still strapped into her seat belt. He checked for vital signs but found none. From the appearance of the body, he thought, she had not been dead for very long. He would later be shocked to learn how wrong he was.

Now Strasser could see that the car had another casualty. Little Nicky was lying nude and curled up in a fetal position in the passenger seat. Strasser sighed and quietly radioed that he'd found the car and two people, deceased. He stared for a moment at the bodies, wishing the outcome had been different. Then he crawled back up the embankment to his unit. He placed some flares in the roadway and flipped on all his vehicle's lights. With nothing to do but wait for help, he gingerly made his way back down the slope again, returning to the wreck for one more look. This time, however, he walked to the passenger side, as painful as he knew that scene would be.

"I looked at Nicky—he was emaciated, like the pictures you see of starving children in third-world countries. He was very bony and had, well, a strange look. From the other side of the car, I hadn't been able to see his face, but now I could see that his eyes were open—that's not unusual when some-one is dead," says Strasser.

Because deputies also act as coroners and are required to confirm deaths, he touched Nicky's neck to check for a pulse. As soon as he did, the child drew a quick, shallow breath. Strasser jumped back. "At first, I thought I was seeing things, so I touched him again—he breathed again! I shouted his name. I got no response, but I kept talking loudly to him, telling him help was coming. I could see then that he started to breathe more normally. He didn't talk or move, just lay there breathing."

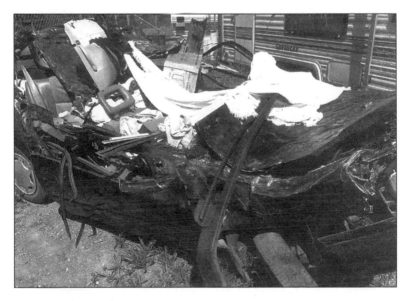

Little Nicky Skubish miraculously survived the accident that demolished his mother's car. (Mountain Democrat)

It took Strasser a moment to compose himself. Now even more impatient for help to arrive, he made a quick assessment of the accident scene. For whatever reason, the car had left the roadway and apparently had done a half-roll to the passenger side when it careened down the embankment. As the car skimmed through the trees on its way down the hill, the roof was peeled back like a sardine tin on Nicky's side of the car. Strasser shuddered at the thought of what might have happened had the child been taller. But an even more incredible realization now dawned on Strasser. Nicky's emaciated condition was probably the result of being without food or water for several days, meaning that the crash must have occurred much longer ago than he first believed.

Paramedics and rescue workers finally arrived to take Nicky to the University of California Davis Medical Center. As full daylight set in, everyone now took in the scene. The circumstances defied explanation. It was determined that Christene had died on impact and had been dead for nearly five days, yet her body was in near-perfect condition. Despite wild temperature swings that week from daytime highs in the 90s to nighttime lows in the 40s, Christene's body showed no signs of the extensive decomposition that normally would have occurred. There were no insects or maggots around the body, and none of the foul odor usually associated with body decay. Instead, rescue personnel noted a strange, sweet odor in the air surrounding Christene's body.

"One theory was that the sweet aroma was from her cologne or some kind of lotion, but after that many days, that's really unlikely," says Strasser, still in awe. "It's almost as though the condition of her body was preserved to make things easier for her son. In his mind, he thought his mom was just asleep."

Everyone was baffled. Later reports from medical experts who examined both Nicky and his mother's body shed some light on the events after the crash, but also further deepened the mysteries. Did Deborah Hoyt actually see Christene Skubish, who might have left the wreckage, climbed up the embankment, and fallen at the roadside while trying to get help? How could that have been possible as experts now were certain that Christene had died on impact five days before? Even if they were wrong about that, says Strasser, it's still beyond reasoning to think she had left the car.

"Based on the extent of her injuries, it's highly unlikely that she unbelted herself, stripped off her clothes, climbed to the road, and lay down for a while—then went back to the car, got dressed, and belted herself back into the seat. Five days after the crash, that just doesn't . . . " Strasser's voice trails off, unable to find the right words.

Was it Nicky? There was evidence that the child had left the car during the week. His seat belt had been on at the time of impact, says Strasser, but was undone when he was found. Poison oak rashes on his body indicate that he had gotten out of the car and moved around. A patch of the plant was found about seven feet away from the vehicle. He had taken off his clothes at some point, probably because of the heat, but was unable to dress himself again later due to his physical condition. Still, Strasser and others insist, Nicky couldn't possibly have been the roadside wraith.

"I say that's impossible. A healthy person would have a very difficult time climbing up that embankment, and by the time Deborah Hoyt had seen someone there, Nicky never would have been able to move. In fact, I had found him only three hours after her sighting. The doctors who saw Nicky said if I hadn't found him when I did, he would have been dead within another hour."

Dead within an hour—Strasser couldn't get over those words. With thoughts of his own children in his head, he had to keep emotions at bay. "I felt really badly for Nicky. The first thing I wanted to do was grab him, hold him, and run for help, but my emergency training stopped me from doing that," he says. "I covered him and kept him warm while the whole situation hit home. I also knew that Christene's family by now had come up from Los Angeles with plans to search for her themselves. They were aware of what route she'd taken, and, for all I knew, they were driving up right behind me. I didn't want them to stumble on this scene, so I had to be ready." Sure enough, the family showed up at the scene, and Strasser had to pull Christene's sister away from the site so she wouldn't see the pair inside the wrecked car.

Strasser ponders the case that was both a tragedy and a triumph. While the family celebrated Nicky's rescue, they mourned Christene's death. Yet it could have been worse had it not been for the apparition on the roadway that finally drew attention to the wrecked car. Deborah Hoyt strongly believes it was some kind of spirit sent by God. Strasser is still trying to explain it within his own beliefs.

"Personally, I believe in heaven, and I believe in angels. It's absolutely not beyond my own beliefs to consider that something supernatural may have happened that night," he admits. Was the road apparition the ghost of a protective mother? A guardian angel? Whatever it was, even if it wasn't there physically, it compelled Deborah Hoyt to call 911—and because of that, little Nicky is alive today.

The Barracks

Just outside of Berkeley Springs, West Virginia, sits a small, quiet neighborhood on US 522. Businesses and residences commingle on the well-traveled highway—an insurance office or two, an ice cream stand, some nice homes, and one particularly attractive brick house. The house's former owner, Ercel Michael, a carpenter, had applied his considerable skills to build his brick home. When he retired, he directed his meticulous efforts toward maintaining all of his property. Neighbors and relatives say he loved taking care of his lawn and was tidy almost to a fault—"a place for everything and everything in its place" was his way.

In 1973, Ercel Michael passed away, and his lovely two-story brick home—with three bedrooms, beautiful hardwood floors, a basement, and an attic—was sold within a year. The new owners appreciated how well the house had been built and planned to put it to good use. But they also had some renovations in mind that Ercel Michael wouldn't have appreciated. And apparently he didn't.

The new owners were the West Virginia State Police, who turned Ercel Michael's house into a small, three-person barracks for their troopers. It was and still is the only state police station in rural Morgan County. In the fall of 1977, not long before Sergeant Jim Riffle was transferred to his second duty station at Berkeley Springs, the police made their biggest renovation to the property: they bulldozed and paved over Ercel Michael's precious, perfect lawn. Soon after the construction, eerie happenings began to occur in the barracks that continue today, occurrences many former and current troopers feel is Mr. Michael himself expressing displeasure at what they've done to his property.

"I think we upset him a bit," says Sergeant Jim Riffle, chuckling. Riffle lived in the barracks full time for six months, sometimes sharing the house with two other troopers, but all the time sharing it with, he believes, Ercel Michael. Now a district commander in nearby Marlington, Riffle recalls a barrage of annoying sounds and other pesky happenings that began not long after he moved in.

"I would come home to the barracks late at night from patrol and find all the lights on inside the house when they had definitely been turned off before I'd left. During the night, I'd hear footsteps of someone coming up the stairs and walking into the bedroom across the hall. Doors were always slamming shut rather loudly," says Riffle.

In fact, the first incident he experienced was a second-floor interior door slamming forcefully right in his face. Riffle was entering a bedroom when suddenly . . . WHAM! "I didn't

The haunted West Virginia State Police barracks in Berkeley Springs, West Virginia (COURTESY OF TODD HARLESS)

know what to think, but I didn't get much sleep that night," he recalls. "I just tried to put it in the back of my mind. But then I'd hear footsteps, and it would really get me wondering." Other troopers at the house also heard the noises, but all swore they were not making them. Riffle admits to being terrified when he first got there. Of course, the other troopers would laugh and tell him to please not make Ercel angry.

Ercel also liked to type. When Riffle's brother came to visit for a few days and stayed with him at the barracks, he heard typewriters clacking away in the downstairs office in the middle of the night. Riffle was the only trooper living in the barracks at the time, but he thought perhaps a fellow trooper had slipped in late to catch up on some reports. But the next day, nothing was disturbed, and other troopers swore they had not stopped by during the night.

"After a while, you just got used to it and didn't think anything about it. It didn't happen all the time, just occasionally," Riffle says. "We always tried to come up with other explanations for the noises and such, but I've been in old houses where there are drafts and doors slamming, and this was different. There were too many different incidents."

After Riffle bought his own house and moved out, Trooper Preston Gooden moved in and managed about two days of peace before being introduced to his ghostly "roommate." Currently the sheriff of neighboring Berkeley County, Gooden lived in the barracks for a year. He also remembers Ercel's penchant for typing.

One night after a late patrol, a weary Gooden headed upstairs to bed. He was alone in the house as Riffle had already left to go home after his shift. Just as Gooden settled into bed, he was jolted by the sound of the office typewriters. Gooden thought at first that Riffle had come back to type something, or worse, he may have run into an accident and maybe Gooden should know about it, too. "I got up and went downstairs to see what had happened, but as soon as I got to the bottom of the stairs, the typewriters just stopped. I looked into the office and it was empty—all the typewriters had their covers over them, and no one was there," he recalls.

Puzzled and uneasy, Gooden went back to bed. It wasn't long before he heard more noises—a strange "thump . . . thump . . . thump . . . " sound made its way ominously up the stairs. At the top landing, the slow thumping noises seemed to head into the bedroom across the hall. Again Gooden checked the house and found himself to be completely alone.

The next day, when he talked with troopers and other employees, Gooden was told about Ercel Michael. A secretary who had known Ercel said the man walked with a walker, which is just what the odd thumping noise had sounded like to Gooden—someone using a walker to get up the stairs. "She said the bedroom, where I heard the noise go after the stairway, had been Ercel's bedroom."

Gooden admits to a short period of anxiety after that. He had difficulty sleeping and was even wary of going upstairs. Then one night Gooden was awakened by a tremendous slam, as though someone had kicked in the back door. Thinking it might be someone breaking in, someone who believed the troopers stored confiscated drugs in the house, Gooden rolled out of bed and grabbed his gun.

"It scared the hell out of me. It wasn't just a bang, it was a *horrendous* bang," he says. "I flew downstairs with my weapon drawn, but no one was there, and everything was perfectly secure. Now I was *really* irritated."

The petty annoyances continued. When Gooden left on patrol he would secure the house and make sure all the lights were out. But when he'd get home, every light in the barracks was blazing again. Then one night, Ercel pulled out all the stops. Besides hearing the walker thumping on the stairs, Gooden cringed at the continuous loud banging of a downstairs door, as though it was slamming in the wind. He went to secure the door, but it was locked tight. He crawled back in bed and the door-slamming started again, as well as more banging in the adjoining bedroom.

Gooden had had enough. "It was really getting on my nerves because I had to get up early the next day for work. I thought, bullcrap, nothing like this can hurt you, you know? I finally went into the hallway and yelled angrily, 'Shut the hell up!' And it all stopped!" For about an hour afterward, Gooden heard a cautious thump here and a soft bump there, but he was at least able to fall asleep. Ercel must have got the message. "From then on, I didn't have it too bad. I'd hear it occasionally, but I got so I just ignored it. It was really weird, though."

Troopers who have lived in the barracks say that Ercel's annoyances were really just that—pesky annoyances, all harmless. Perhaps his antics were meant to frighten off the troopers, but if so, they didn't work. Everyone got used to the house's eccentricities and mostly ignored them, continuing with day-to-day life and work as usual. The only one who apparently couldn't get used to the situation was Ercel Michael. Over the years, the incidents kept happening, and the troopers kept ignoring them for the most part. Today, no one lives at the barracks full time, though troopers on night-call duty will sleep over. This arrangement is apparently still unsatisfactory to Ercel. Current Detachment Commander Sergeant W. D. "Deke" Walker is a bit more skeptical than his predecessors, but he admits the noises continue. His troopers mostly make light of it.

"I don't want to sound like my troopers are frightened. Guys hear something, they get worked up in their mind if it's something they can't explain. They'll say they've had an 'Ercel experience.' But it's really more of a joking type thing when we talk about the old man who used to live here," Walker says. "I don't believe in it myself. There's no rattling chains, but I go along with them. I did have a problem finding someone to stay overnight here last Halloween, though."

Ercel's relatives don't believe he is haunting the house, either, and say he would never harm anyone. He liked police officers, they point out, and was a very gentle man. Walker believes that wholeheartedly and then admits to having heard the noises himself. He doesn't worry about explaining them and feels if he took the time to look, he'd find a logical explanation. "I've told people that Ercel and I sat down, had a beer and talked, and that was the end of it—he's never bothered me again," he says, tongue placed firmly in cheek.

But it seems that Ercel has expanded his repertoire beyond his old favorite noises and has added harmless interference with patrol vehicles. A trooper couldn't get the electric windows in his cruiser to function properly, until he patiently asked Ercel to please leave him alone for a while. The windows promptly operated once again. Walker has even asked Ercel to be quiet on occasion. "I've got a pretty good group of guys here. If something happens that they can't readily explain or don't want to explain, they just blame it on Ercel. If they want to do that, I say fine."

Riffle isn't surprised that the "haunting" continues, nor is he bothered by the reaction of others to his tales.

"I try to be lighthearted about it. I know people look at me like I'm nuts and laugh, but I'll tell you—I was there," he states with certainty. "I know what I saw and heard over the

12 years I was stationed in that area, and it's not beyond my realm of belief to think that it's a restless spirit. There's just no other explanation for it."

So the troopers and Ercel Michael—or whatever it is—continue to coexist in relative peace. Opinions are divided almost equally between those who believe the noises are just the creaking and settling of an old house and those who think Ercel never forgave them for paving over his beautiful lawn. Perhaps the lawn has little to do with it, and Ercel may simply want some privacy in his own home. Although the state troopers have sometimes called Ercel Michael an undesired houseguest, it's quite possible that the unwanted visitors are the troopers themselves.

2

PSYCHIC
PHENOMENA

POLICE OFFICERS ARE DIVIDED on the issue of accepting help from psychics on tough cases, but not equally divided. For as many cops as I found who said they give consideration to psychic tips, I found far more who said it's all so much hooey. They say the information received from these "soothsayers" is vague at best and certainly would be laughed out of court—if any one were crazy enough to try using it in court. Besides, if a psychic can't say to them, "You'll find the body buried 10 feet west of the signpost at the northeast corner of Main and Seventh," what's the use?

For the most part, psychic impressions are usually just nebulous enough that police can't act on the information directly. They solve the crime through conventional methods and sometimes discover after the fact that a psychic was in the ballpark, if not uncannily accurate. There have been incidents, however, in which psychic tips caused police to consider other directions for their investigations that they might not have considered before. Sometimes that change in direction led to solving the crime. In such cases, was the psychic's information actually the key factor? Although most cops wouldn't come out and say that it was, the possibility is difficult to ignore.

There are other ways that psychic information might be used to a cop's advantage. Several investigators have said that if psychic impressions are found to agree with aspects of their case, it sometimes helps provide a sense of certainty about those aspects. Some cops find that validation very useful, particularly if the information is coming from a psychic they know and trust and who has been accurate in the past.

One investigator in Tempe, Arizona, found psychic predictions to be helpful in an offbeat way. In the case of a murdered young woman, the victim's roommate claimed to have no idea who might have been involved. But when Detective Al Reed played for her an audiotape of a psychic's predictions, he got a different story.

"The prediction was that the roommate would be the next victim," says Reed. "She apparently believed in psychics and became afraid. She had suspicions that her boyfriend might have been involved in the murder, but never said anything to us. Hearing the tape may have helped her express the suspicions she brushed off before."

In Reed's case, a worker had found the victim's body in a canal filtration system. Earlier, the psychic had described the location where the body would be found, and that description turned out to be remarkably accurate. But later visions proved to be way off base—so far off that police lost all faith in that particular psychic's abilities.

Cops will admit to feeling chills any time a psychic's information is extremely accurate. But such visions just don't hit the nail on the head every time. If they're not detailed enough to help police find the body, the missing person, or the killer, do they really mean anything? Can extrasensory perception ever be of consistent, practical use? Apparently the U.S. government thought so, because for many years it quietly pumped a lot of money into secret psychic research for intelligence gathering. It called the process "remote viewing."

The U.S. Government's "Remote Viewers"

Although law enforcement has only recently begun to talk more openly about the use of psychics in criminal investigations, research and practical use of remote viewing have been going on for over 20 years in the spy community. ESP has been a part of espionage since the early 1970s, when the Central Intelligence Agency (CIA) first saw the fascinating possibilities of the mind as another tool in a spy's bag of tricks. The fact that the Soviet Union was already using remote viewers for spying duties—with the United States as its primary psychic target—is what really propelled the CIA into starting their own research. In the Cold War atmosphere of "do unto the other guy the same thing he's doing to you," our government felt there must be at least *some* substance to extrasensory perception. It quickly assembled a team of psychics to begin research into the phenomenon and to find practical applications for it.

Eventually the remote viewer research project was turned over to the Defense Intelligence Agency (DIA). With the still-interested CIA watching dutifully over its shoulder, DIA began its top-secret remote viewing programs, such as Project Stargate, which used both military and civilian remote viewers. Over a 20-year period, thousands of experiments were conducted. Remote viewers were called upon to assist with various duties that ranged from locating U.S. hostages in foreign countries to foreseeing an accidental attack on a U.S. naval vessel. And all of these experiments were done from the comfort of a small, white-walled room.

But this was just the type of project that pundits of wasteful government spending were thrilled to sink their teeth into. In mid-1995, Congress commissioned the American Institutes for Research to conduct a review of the $20 million Stargate program to assess its usefulness, specifically the practicality of remote viewing applied to intelligence gathering. One conclusion drawn in the resulting report, *An Evaluation of Remote Viewing: Research and Applications*, by Drs. Michael Mumford, Andrew M. Rose, and David A. Goslin, was blunt and to the point:

> Remote viewing, as exemplified by the efforts in the current program, has not been shown to have value in intelligence operations. . . . Continued support for the operational component of the current program is not justified.

These statements reflect the reviewers' belief that the program did not show unequivocally that remote viewing could even be done. Although they agreed that significant results were seen in laboratory experiments of remote viewing, they weren't sure just what was responsible for those results. The reviewers concluded that "at this juncture it would be premature to assume that we have a convincing demonstration of a paranormal phenomenon." But they went on to add that, "This is not to say definitively that paranormal phenomena do not exist."

In other words, they're not sure. Something happened, but they don't know why. Though the results didn't prove that extrasensory perception exists, they also didn't prove that it *doesn't* exist. What the phenomenon of remote viewing means and how useful it might be is still anyone's guess. We're right back to square one. The U.S. government now says that it's out of the psychic spy business and that the programs have been shut down. But one former DIA psychological consultant and remote viewer believes the research should continue. He feels that we are beginning to understand this phenomenon and eventually will find practical uses for it.

"The remote viewing research programs had some very

encouraging and suggestive results, enough that I think it warrants further very intensive research into this area of psychology," says Dr. Keith Harary, a northern California psychologist and long-time researcher into the phenomenon he prefers to call *extended perception*. In 1980, Harary was invited to participate in the first civilian remote-viewing research programs for the CIA, and later became part of the Project Stargate team for several years.

"I think that the discontinuation of projects like Stargate is tragic. The program had great potential—they had a tiger by the tail and the tiger got away. But it's still out there wandering around."

Harary is trying to move the phenomenon away from the "psychic stuff" that conjures up images of flamboyant fortune-tellers toward what goes on in the human mind that produces this kind of extended perception. To bring it into the mainstream of science, he says, shifts it toward understanding how certain perceptual processes work in the brain. "I don't believe it does anybody any good to look at this as paranormal. It's straight perceptual psychology and not a paranormal phenomenon, in my opinion," he states.

This is not a popular viewpoint on several fronts. For one, it implies that extended perception is not necessarily a special gift. Harary doesn't believe that it makes any sense to think of extended perception as something some human beings have and others don't. It's either a real human process or it isn't, he says. There are those, however, who perpetuate what he calls the myth of psychic privilege, the idea that "I'm a psychic . . . and you're not." When one considers the potential economic benefits of being a psychic when others aren't—just check the long list of credit-card-accepting psychic telephone hotlines—it becomes apparent why the notion of being privileged has its own rewards.

"I was once told that I'm missing the chance to make a lot of money by holding to my belief that everyone has the ability to hone extended perception," Harary says candidly. "And much to my continuing dismay, I am often labeled a psychic by people who know that I abhor the term."

Certainly the concept of extended perception as science would make it more palatable to those who shy away because of the fortune-teller image. Along that line, police might feel more comfortable working with a *scientist* as opposed to a *psychic*.

Psychics and Criminal Investigators

The term *psychic* is still commonly used, however. In the area of law enforcement, the word can still cause officers to run as fast as they can in the opposite direction. The whole area of psychic prediction tends to have a kind of kooky public image, because often kooky people are attracted to it. This tendency creates a self-perpetuating cycle that can make it difficult for a scientist investigating the field to be taken seriously. When psychics become involved in police cases, the kooky connotations can create a real circus atmosphere. That image can be a public relations headache for any law enforcement agency.

At a certain level, however, it seems that some law enforcement authorities aren't necessarily bothered by appearances. Psychic assistance could be called a *black box* for all they care. They want to solve crimes, period. And if psychic assistance helps them solve a case, that's enough for them. Others can ponder and speculate about the hows and whys all they want; in the end, they're just happy they got the bad guy. The problem arises when psychics—solicited or unsolicited—interfere with catching the bad guy by delaying investigators and wasting time and resources. Then police are not going to be happy.

This problem is especially true in high-profile cases, which tend to attract psychics. Whether the tipsters are famous or unknown, kooky or sincere, their sheer numbers can result in a massive waste of time and resources for an agency that's likely under enormous pressure to solve a crime quickly. One case in point was the 1993 abduction and murder of 12-year-old Polly Klaas, a crime that horrified her hometown of Petaluma, California, and the nation as a whole.

"In the 65 days between Polly's abduction and the discovery of her body, more than 5,000 unsolicited calls came into authorities from would-be psychics," says Keith Harary. "This overwhelmed the resources of the people trying to break this case. With that many calls, how do you separate the good information from the bad? More important, how do you find the time and manpower to even bother?"

The callers were sincere people who wanted to do good and who really felt they knew something about the case. They had seen all the TV and newspaper reports and would start getting pictures in their heads, says Harary. Everyone wanted to get the perpetrator as much as the police did. When the call went out to the general public asking for any information concerning the case, anyone with a hunch picked up the phone and called the police. The tipsters didn't mean any harm, but they did overwhelm the law enforcement people who were trying to save the little girl. Checking out every single lead was simply exhausting and wasted precious time. According to the Petaluma police, some of the psychic leads were patently ridiculous, but *all* led to dead ends. Yet each tip had to be checked out because there was always the feeling that no stone should be left unturned, just in case the snake happened to be under one of them.

Now imagine dealing with that volume of calls in a one-week period. After the murder of fashion designer Gianni Versace in Miami Beach in July 1997, thousands of calls from citizens and psychics alike poured into tip hotlines nationwide when authorities announced that the prime suspect in the killing was Andrew Cunanan, a man alleged to have committed four other murders. Cunanan was "seen" in nearly all 50 states, as well as in many callers' psychic visions. According to the FBI's Miami field office, their local hotline alone logged more than 1,000 calls. And the Dade County, Florida, Crime-stoppers line took 2,000 tips.

In the end, Cunanan committed suicide after he was accidentally discovered holed up in a houseboat moored off Miami Beach's North Beach section. It appeared Cunanan had been on his floating hideaway for at least a few days before he was discovered, yet none of the tips—psychic or otherwise—focused on the now-famous blue houseboat. One psychic did, however, mention a boat.

"The psychic who called us said Cunanan was on a boat, but do you know how many boats there are in Florida?" says Sergeant John Roper of Dade County Crimestoppers. "I told her that she should call back if she could tell me exactly what the name of the boat was and exactly where it was located. She didn't call back."

Another problem: it's not possible for authorities to know exactly where the caller is getting the information. It could be the result of some logical deductive process or simply good guessing. It could be something of a truly extended perceptual nature. Or, as occasionally happens, the caller could be someone directly involved in the crime, even the perpetrator himself. With that thought, the innocent caller could become a suspect. Unless the caller has some good connections to the law enforcement agency and plenty of people to vouch for his or her character and integrity, trying to help could bring more trouble than the would-be psychic anticipated.

If authorities actually do want to seek out this type of extraordinary help, however, it can be difficult to find someone they can rely on for good information based on extended perception. Putting out a blind call can often attract people who are out to promote themselves, looking to charge big money and to acquire a big reputation. The truly sincere people may not answer the call. All in all, it's still a roll of the dice, and the whole process must be undertaken with great care. Yet it seems that more police agencies are indeed testing the waters.

At the Office of Paranormal Investigations in Orinda, California, director Loyd Auerbach says calls are on the rise from law enforcement agencies seeking information on how to work with psychics.

"Police want to know the best way to ask questions of a psychic. They want to know about the ego involved and what to expect in general," he reports. "They are asking for help because they don't really know how or if it works. My experience has been that if they take too much of a skeptical standpoint, very often they end up providing pieces of the puzzle to the psychic. That's self-defeating."

Perhaps people who call themselves psychics are just wired differently and therefore think differently. For instance, the missing pieces of a case may not be obvious to those working on it, but they could be to a psychic. Are psychics culling information from somewhere else, or are they merely taking an intuitive leap, pulling together information that *is* there but that they are somehow better equipped to correlate?

"Einstein made an intuitive leap that most people could not make—he was wired differently," says Auerbach. "So was Isaac Newton. If psychics called themselves problem solvers or consultants, they'd probably have more success in getting police to work with them. There would be less skepticism about receiving their information."

Some of that skepticism seems to be fading, though. It appears that when police develop a certain comfort level with a particular psychic, that's when the whole process works best. Finding that reliable person is the most difficult part. But maybe police are looking in the wrong places.

Do-It-Yourself Perception

If psychic privilege is a myth and everyone really does have untapped extended perception capabilities, why don't police just develop their own psychic ability? This idea isn't completely unheard of, but it's rarely verbalized in that way. Cops always talk about their gut-level feelings. A former Seattle police officer told me: "I have found that the best detectives and patrol officers work on their gut instincts, the old seat-of-the-pants feeling." These feelings are not consciously developed; they tend to be the result of years of experience on the streets. In general, people are taught to discount their own perceptions. But on top of that, cops are analytical by training and often by nature.

"If we totally discounted our analytic functioning, we couldn't survive in the world," says Keith Harary. "What would be truly helpful is to learn how to allow *some* of the less tangible intuitive impressions to be acknowledged without getting too carried away."

Consciously choosing to go with intuitions and perceptions could pose several problems. Developing one's extended perception to the point of being useful takes practice. A requirement for practice would be finding opportunities to work with this perception in real-world situations without interfering with normal investigative procedures. In police work, those conditions are truly hard to find. That's why authorities tend to stick with the tried and true tools. But if an officer is exceptionally stable mentally and emotionally and is willing to incorporate some extended perception information for use in conjunction with other information, is there really anything wrong with that?

There might be if a cop begins to have too many hunches. It wouldn't do to have an officer who is suddenly afraid to make a move because of a hunch that something is behind a wall when there really isn't anything there. And just what is a hunch anyway? Having a head full of information and analysis about a crime could be counterproductive when trying to crack a case intuitively. What an officer thinks is an intuitive impression is more likely to be a combination of all those analytic points.

"He can't get the mental noise out of his head. Therefore, he must go to someone who really knows nothing about the situation and then not tell that person very much at all,"

Harary explains. "This is how things were done in Project Stargate. In most cases, all I was told was, 'We have a situation.' " Police then need to see if the psychic's information relates accurately to what is already known about the case. If so, then they can feel more comfortable about the information they give to the psychic that doesn't relate to anything known outside the squad room. If the officer himself is trying to use intuition, he's missing that reliability check."

What's really needed is to find a way to sift correct information from incorrect information. A person doesn't have to be correct all the time, as long as there is a way to determine what's accurate and what isn't about their impressions. It may sound almost impossible, but the only way to approach the problem is through ongoing perceptual research, including neurophysiological research. At this point, not only don't we know what percentage of our brains we use, we're not even sure what all the areas of the brain actually do.

"Neuroscience is a very new field. We have by no means figured out the brain or perception. So it just doesn't make sense to say that things can or can't be a certain way," says Harary.

"I'd like to work with police departments, the FBI, and other law enforcement agencies to help them hone their *own* extended perception capabilities. But unfortunately, none of this is reliable enough yet to bottle and turn into a permanent part of the law enforcement arsenal."

The next sections present some interesting cases involving cops and psychics in which the police met with some success, learned a lot, and reconsidered their previously held notions. In "Heavy Psi," a homicide investigator finds himself adrift in a sea of psychics when one of their own researchers is brutally murdered. "The Cop and the Psychic" is the story of a detective who solves his murder case and discovers there might actually be more to psychic abilities than he thought. We also look at Native American spiritualism as Navajo police call upon the old ways to assist their investigations in "Ancient Medicine."

Heavy Psi

An out-of-body experience as a teenager drew D. Scott Rogo into the world of the paranormal. So remarkable was the incident that it led him to his life's work of exploring the science of such phenomena as telepathy, clairvoyance, and extrasensory perception. By the time he was 40, Rogo had become well known and respected in the field of parapsychology as an investigator, lecturer, and author, with 30 books to his credit. Friends describe the suburban Los Angeles man as someone who was generous and willing to help strangers, but whose life revolved around one consuming passion: Scott Rogo wanted to know what becomes of a person's mind and soul after death.

Rogo was utterly absorbed by the subject and driven to the difficult task of researching centuries-old literature about life after death. He uncovered every account he could find that described people's personal experiences of receiving messages from beyond the grave. Although he desperately wanted to understand what those incidents meant, colleagues say he never manipulated his research to fit his theories. Rogo wanted to find the *real* answer and would never claim to know the truth if he couldn't prove it.

On August 16, 1990, Scott Rogo involuntarily learned the real answer.

A neighbor became suspicious when he noticed that Rogo's backyard sprinkler had been running continuously for two days. He summoned police, who entered the house and found Rogo's bloody body. He had been viciously stabbed to death.

Los Angeles Police Department investigators first suspected robbery as a motive for the killing. A stereo, VCR, and other items were missing from Rogo's home, but there were no signs of forced entry—a clue that the murderer was possibly someone Rogo had known. It also appeared that more than one person had been involved. As the crime unit collected blood samples, fingerprints, and other evidence, Detective Tim Moss leafed through Rogo's personal address book, hoping to find clues to the killer's identity. Then began the long process of interviewing people who knew Rogo, starting with those under "A" in the book.

Moss didn't have to go beyond "B" before he found a suspect. When he interviewed John Battista, who had known Rogo for several years, the man told a story about the night in question that made Moss suspicious.

"Battista's girlfriend was his alibi, but their stories were inconsistent. We took the girlfriend aside and worked on that, and then the story fell apart," says Moss. "It was highly likely that Battista was at Rogo's house at the time of the murder."

Canvasing some nightclubs that Rogo had frequented, Moss soon found a bartender who recalled seeing the victim and another man together the night of the murder. The bartender described Rogo's companion well enough for a police artist to create a composite sketch. The face was "almost like a photo of John Battista," says Moss. But all he had done was place the two men together at the bar. Questioning Battista further yielded nothing, and there was no physical evidence linking him to the crime scene.

The department's Scientific Investigations Division (SID) had found two fingerprints at the house—one on a drinking glass and a single bloody fingerprint on a wall next to the body. SID had said the print on the glass wasn't good enough to run through the computer for a positive match to Battista or anyone else. The bloody print had a problem as well.

"The single bloody fingerprint turned out to be from someone's little finger, and that's the only print that's not put into the computer system," says Moss. "That particular print is rarely found without other prints, so, in order to gain 20 percent more computer space, it's not cataloged."

With no solid evidence against Battista, Moss couldn't go forward with any charges. Detectives had to look elsewhere for the killers. Moss says Rogo had rented his garage to a man police knew as a drug dealer. There happened to be two major investigations of that dealer's activities going on at the time. Perhaps a few of the man's many customers had singled out

Rogo as a target for robbery. Also, cryptic gang-style writings were found on sidewalks and the back wall of Rogo's house—another possible lead.

"There were so many different things going on in this case, we were running in circles and went off on about 20 different tangents," Moss says. "All of them proved to be false leads. But the more we learned about Battista, the more everything kept coming back to him, even though his fingerprints had been eliminated as a suspect's."

The situation was complicated by a mountain of tips from civilians. Because of Rogo's prominence in the parapsychology field, it wasn't long before psychics from around the world began writing letters and calling the LAPD with their visions of the murder. Moss was overwhelmed both by the sheer number of tips and by a particularly heavy caseload at the time, but he wasn't about to turn away any potentially helpful information. He enlisted the help of a close friend of Rogo's, Betty Bandy, who volunteered to sift through the psychics' predictions. She created a chart to record their readings. Moss was fascinated by the fact that many of the psychics were confirming much of what he already knew.

"A lot of the information was incredibly accurate in areas these people couldn't have known about," he says. "Many of them described Battista and also the second suspect. But no one provided any clues to the second man's identity—at least not at that point."

Moss was still bothered by the fingerprint found on the drinking glass. He strongly believed the print was good and couldn't understand why SID had been unable to process it well enough to be useful. Also, new information made him even more eager to recheck that print. Rogo's friends and family had told Moss that Rogo was a compulsive housekeeper, the type who would wash dirty dishes and glasses the moment someone was finished with them. If a used glass was sitting on the coffee table, they said, Rogo would have picked it up and taken it to the kitchen right away—if he wasn't already dead.

If that were so, Moss reasoned then the glass police found could have been used by one of the killers.

Convinced that the print would be valuable, Moss went back to SID and argued his position that it should be processed again by a different expert. SID reluctantly agreed, and the print was sent to another agency. While it was being reworked, Moss got a call from Betty Bandy. She had received an audiotape prediction from a psychic named Armand Marcotte, who used meditation and astrological information to draw a conclusion that would prove surprisingly correct.

"Marcotte said that one of the suspects left something behind at the scene that should be traceable to that person," says Moss. "He said the killers had got a drink and that there should be an empty glass in the house. Marcotte was sure the glass would have a fingerprint on it even though the killers had been careful. It was really eerie since nothing about the print on the glass had been released in the press."

Both Moss and Marcotte were right. The fingerprint from the glass was indeed usable and came back a positive make on John Battista. By now, however, Battista had disappeared, and the detectives launched a search for him. Meanwhile, Moss was contacted by another psychic who, instead of providing information, wanted his help with a different case.

Donna Ryan*, at the suggestion of a mutual friend, called Moss to vent her frustration. An investigator on a separate case had brushed off her attempts to provide information about the crime. She asked if Moss would intervene on her behalf. Not wishing to barge in on another detective's case, Moss declined. His refusal didn't stop Ryan from dropping by the station unannounced soon afterward. When she arrived, Moss had been searching unsuccessfully for his lost cellular phone and was somewhat irritated.

"Donna was talking about all this psychic stuff, and I finally said, 'Look, if you really are one of these psychics, tell me where my damned cell phone is,'" Moss recalls. "She thought about it for a moment, then told me it wasn't lost and that I'd find it lying on a tag within 10 minutes." A tag? Ryan tugged at Moss's jacket, which was draped over the back of his chair, and pointed to the label sewn into the neckline.

"I said, 'Oh yeah, sure.' I looked around for another 10 minutes, then went back outside to my car," Moss continues. "I opened the door and my raincoat was lying on the front seat. I said, 'Nah, it can't be.' I carefully opened the coat, and there was the phone, lying on the tag. It gave me the chills."

After that incident, Moss felt there was nothing to lose by asking Ryan for her impressions on the Rogo case. On a subsequent visit to the house, she accompanied him. As Ryan sat on the front steps, she described a scenario in which two men had visited Rogo. Interestingly, she agreed with many of the other psychics who had said the men wanted money. Because Rogo kept almost none in the house, they became angry and killed him, she said. Yet Ryan focused most on a man who wasn't present at the crime, but whom she felt knew all the details. She provided Moss with the man's first name.

"Donna said that Battista and this man were good friends, that they looked very much alike and called each other 'brother,' but they weren't really brothers," says Moss. "She told me the man's first name was either Joseph* or Robert*, and that he knew all about what had happened. So I talked again with people who knew Battista to try to find out who this guy was. I learned Battista did indeed have a friend who looked just like him, and they did call each other 'brother'— a friend named Joseph Roberts. I couldn't believe it. Donna was right on the mark with that one."

Battista was finally located and Roberts was picked up for questioning. Both men refused to cooperate and would not name the third murder suspect, who had long since fled. No one knew where he was, and although police had some suspicions about who he might be, they were not sure. Allegedly the third suspect was the one who actually killed Rogo while Battista simply sat and watched.

"Rogo had given both men a drink of water, then cleaned

up all the glasses except Battista's because he wasn't finished yet. The suspects soon started an argument about money," says Moss. "They wanted money, but Rogo never kept any at his house. I think they were disappointed—here was this big-time author with no money around. The second suspect picked up a kitchen knife and started stabbing Rogo and chasing him through the house. I don't think Battista took part in the stabbing, but he sure covered up for the other guy and didn't lift a finger to stop him. Then they grabbed the stereo, the VCR, and some other items and left."

John Battista eventually was charged and convicted of second-degree murder. Joseph Roberts was not charged. Interestingly, Battista's first trial ended in a hung jury, partly due to the composite sketch, says Moss. "Roberts and Battista looked so much alike that the defense argued the sketch was really Roberts. But Battista was convicted in a retrial." The case has been cleared even though the third murder suspect is still at large. Police believe he is a person who has an extremely common name like "John Smith," and because of that, says Moss, it's been next to impossible to track him down.

Why can't the psychics who were so accurate in the early stages of the case now locate "John Smith"? No one knows. But despite the lack of consistency in the psychic tips in this case, Moss still does not discount such information.

"I'm the type of person who doesn't turn away *any* information. I think psychic tips are very useful, I really do, if you've got no leads to go on," he says. "It doesn't hurt, that's for sure. If you use it for what it is and don't try to build a case on it, I think it's a helpful tool if used with all the other investigative tools."

For someone who was so consumed with what happens to people after death, it's ironic that Scott Rogo died prematurely. But he was so prolific in his writing and research that he effectively crammed an entire lifetime of work into a short period. One of the many books Rogo wrote is titled *Phone Calls from the Dead*, in which he seriously investigated accounts of those who claim the deceased have reached out and touched them in that manner. Detective Tim Moss bought the book and found it interesting, to say the least.

He's also kept a close eye on his cellular phone ever since.

The Cop and the Psychic

(Detective Robert W. Lee, Lake Oswego, Oregon, Police Department, as told to the author)

I'm what they call a left-brained thinker. I'm real good with things I can see, touch, feel, or prove with science. Mr. Details. I'm very good with numbers and computers, and if I wasn't a cop, I'd probably be an accountant or some sort of a businessman.

The right side of my brain, my artistic side, is not so well developed. I've been told I don't even play the radio properly, I have so little musical ability. Actually, I have none at all. Which is OK, since I'm a cop and police work takes left-brain thinking. You deal with the facts and evidence, put pieces of the puzzle together, and usually you get a whole, complete picture. Usually.

In the spring of 1986, I had a picture with a lot of pesky holes in it, a missing persons case that became a homicide real quick. Alexis Sara Burke had disappeared after having an argument with her husband, John. Just up and left without a trace, leaving her disabled child behind. Very unlike her. We interviewed friends and relatives and did lots of exhaustive searches, but I had few solid clues and I sure had a lot of unanswered questions. I was pretty certain I knew what happened, though. Just why *did* John get rid of every one of his wife's possessions within days of her disappearance? That's really unusual. He said they were planning to divorce, and she was going to move out anyway, but it still didn't feel right. I was certain John had killed her—all I had to do was prove it.

The challenge to my left brain came when the victim's family told me they'd brought in a psychic to help them figure out what was going on. A psychic. I think you see the problem here. My impression of what a psychic was going to be was a little gray-haired old lady wearing purple robes. She'd have a big four-by-eight-foot sheet of plywood stuck in her front yard that says "Madam Melba Reads," with a big handprint on it. You know the type; they're around. But this particular psychic had told the family some key things about my case that only I knew, things I hadn't shared with anyone else. So she'd at least got my attention. We'd had some inquiries in the past from other police agencies about Laurie McQuary. She was a psychic who was known to work with cops once in a while, and she lived and worked here in our town. But my department didn't know anything; we'd never had any contact with her. And I sure hadn't, because it's not my style or my personality to be involved with psychics. So now I wanted to contact Laurie myself for several reasons, the biggest of which was to find out exactly what she knew about my missing person. I also wanted to know *why* she knew it, and, of course, I wanted to find out if she was a nut case.

You're going to find this *very* hard to believe, but sometimes I can be somewhat of a smart-ass. When I phoned Laurie McQuary about setting up a meeting, she almost didn't agree. I think I came off as too "police," though years later Laurie would put it a bit more bluntly to a newspaper reporter: "Detective Lee had an attitude. He was real flip." Perhaps. But when I called, she was having one of those days, like psychics often have. She had been ridiculed; people were condescending, thinking she's out to lunch. So what do I do but call and invite her out to lunch. She finally agreed. I went to her office, and at first I thought I'd gone to the wrong place. It was a *business* office that looked like any other attorney's or accountant's office, with no plywood sign, no palm print. And I was looking at a very attractive, dark-haired lady wearing a dressy, feminine business suit instead of purple robes. Somehow, I felt a *little* bit better.

At a nice restaurant right across the street from her office, we sat on the second-floor balcony, and between bites of ham and turkey sandwiches, Laurie told me 30 things about my case: who, what, when, where, how come, who knew about it, a description of the car used to transport the body, and stuff like that. I was intrigued. Some of what she was saying I did indeed know to be true, and some other things I was almost 100 percent certain about. Laurie said that John had killed his wife, that he strangled her. She also said a whole circle of people around John and his younger brother, Daniel*, knew all about it.

Laurie went on to describe the victim's car, the area where it would be found, and a slew of other things. I tried to take her comments as seriously as I could, but I had one problem: a lot of what she said had to do with Daniel. A law student at a local college, he had been in California playing softball for the school team during the time frame in question. We'd proved that beyond a doubt. So he was pretty much out of the equation, yet Laurie insisted that Daniel had helped John bury his wife. Then she told me where to find the body.

"It's 15 miles southwest of here, near water," she said.

I raised one eyebrow. "This is Oregon, gimme a break! *Everything* is near water!"

OK, so that was flip. But I finished lunch with the idea that we'd check a few places "near water," which we did, as well as try to find a place Laurie had mentioned called Bell's Landing. She said it was significant to the victim. We pored over geological survey maps but found nothing. So I decided she was wrong about that one. After spending four or five days running down some of Laurie's leads and chatting with people she named, we still didn't have anything close to a prosecutable case. We didn't have a body. I was irritated. Laurie worked with me for about a month, then she was off the case, and I was left with her information. What could I do with it? Right or wrong, I knew I had to get a confession out of John, and I thought I knew how to do that.

John was an interesting sort. He used to be a big-time athlete in school, but now at 29 he'd deteriorated into a slovenly couch potato. Incredibly lazy, he was pretty much unemployable by anyone's accepted standards. But he did work at his dad's metal fabrication plant, or at least he did if and when he felt like it. John swore he had no idea where his wife had gone, but he had too much of a "good riddance" attitude about him for my comfort. Everything we knew about John's personality said that if we pressured him enough, he'd tell a lot of people what he'd done. But we had to pressure him indirectly so that he wouldn't tell us to drop off the end of the earth, then get a lawyer and clam up. And if Daniel supposedly knew what was going on, I had to get to him somehow, too. So we talked with the people in their little circle, and we did it a lot—hoping each time we did, they'd tell John.

In fact, I became John's worst nightmare. I'd follow him around, knowing with whom and where he'd be hanging out. I'd walk into bars and restaurants where he'd be, just so I could wave and say, "Hi, John!" We went overboard being nice to his friends, and they were real easy to get along with. This was a homicide investigation, after all, and nobody wanted to buy a piece of it. Well, the pressure worked, and it worked like a charm. John was telling *everyone* what he'd done. Unfortunately, no one was telling *me* about it!

Almost a year passed, and I was still not being told about it. Suddenly one day, I got a nice little note from Laurie, inviting me over for coffee the next time I was in the neighborhood. Out of the blue. We had spent a lot of time together early in the case, and she was a very nice lady—intelligent, attractive—even if she did look at the world in a right-brain kind of way. And we were both single. What the heck. I phoned her and accepted.

"You said last year you'd call me sometime, but you never did," she teased.

"I was *busy!*" I fibbed.

So we met and started spending a lot of time together. It

was great to bounce ideas off her once in a while. The Burke case was complicated. Although Laurie was no longer involved, it helped to talk about it with her in generalities because she looks at things in a substantially different way than I do. I might get so bogged down with one detail that I won't see another, so a different view is always welcome. And Laurie believes that most people, including me, have intuitive abilities just like she does, only most people don't use them or trust them. I prefer to call it gut hunches. I can live with that.

Several months later, I got a phone call from the police in Newberg, Oregon. A man had called them with information they thought I should know. Seems this woman, Peggy Sue Fontana*, who used to live here in Lake Oswego but now lived in Seattle, had told a girlfriend that she once had a boyfriend who had killed his wife. This girlfriend of hers told another girlfriend, who told another girlfriend, who told another girlfriend, who told *another* girlfriend who just *happened* to be this man's daughter. The daughter didn't even know who Peggy Sue was, but she mentioned this story to Dad, who then called the cops. They ran the details through the crime computer, looking for a match of circumstances, and up popped my case. It was fifth-hand talk, they said, but they figured I might be interested. I said thank you very much.

We discovered that Peggy Sue was wanted in Oregon on a felony warrant for theft. We went to Seattle, introduced ourselves to her, and offered to trade away whatever kind of legal problems she had in Oregon for information about her former boyfriend, John Burke, whom she was still in love with. Peggy Sue told us everything she could remember, but we still needed an admission from John. I figured if he'd told her once, perhaps he'd discuss it with her again, so I wanted her to contact him by phone. Problem was, the laws in Washington state wouldn't allow us to record the call surreptitiously. But in Oregon, she could record any call that she was a part of without informing the other party on the line. So we brought Peggy Sue to Oregon, set her up with a phone and recorder, and she called John. Well, the plan worked well enough that we were sure John killed Alexis, but it didn't work enough to take the evidence into a courtroom. See, Peggy Sue was ancient history with John, and he wasn't that thrilled to be talking with her. But he'd said enough to convince us we'd been right all along. There was no more doubt in our minds that John had done it.

But Peggy Sue recalled a few other things that helped us out. One, she remembered that every time she and John drove past a large field next to the plant where he worked, he became very distant. Even though he never told her how he had killed his wife or where he had ditched the body, Peggy Sue had a hunch he'd buried her in that field somewhere. Second, she once had a talk with John's brother Daniel that made her think he knew exactly what had happened. She knew Daniel well enough to know that his roommate, Rufus Krauss*, was probably in on it, as well as Rufus's two former roommates, Andy Teresi* and Baxter Crowe*. This story was suddenly sounding a lot like what Laurie had said when she listed who knew about the murder. Even though they'd all denied knowing anything, it was looking as if Laurie was right. It was time to lay the cards on the table.

I went to Andy Teresi for a little chat. Waving a grand jury subpoena in his face, I rattled off his options, all of which had him going directly to jail without passing Go, except for one: Talk and tell the truth. Now Andy was a law student, so it only took him about 30 seconds to decide that he didn't want anything to do with this. He told me Rufus had bragged about helping John and Daniel bury the body, but that he had nothing to do with the murder itself. I patted him on the head, said my thank-yous, and then went to find Baxter. I offered him the same set of options: Thou shalt go to jail unless thou tellest me everything I want to know. This boy took about 20 seconds to decide that he wanted nothing to do with a homicide because he didn't even know the suspect. His story matched Andy's, so he got a pat on the head.

Now we brought Rufus in for the drill. Rufus, it turned out, was not very bright at all. I don't know how many thousands of dollars in attorney's fees it ended up costing him, but Rufus—tall, muscular, with a great suntan, a ladies' man—is one of those guys who says that whatever you can do, he can do better. He had nothing to do with burying the body, but to make himself a little bit bigger and more important, he interjected himself into this god-awful situation by telling his buddies that he was part of it, too. Why on earth would a person say he was involved in a murder when he really wasn't?! The truth was that John had killed his wife, and only Daniel had helped him bury her. But how could Daniel have done that when he was out of town at the time?

You know, just when you think you've heard and seen it all, you hear one better. As it turned out, John was so helpless without Daniel around that he couldn't even get it together to dispose of Alexis's body by himself. So he stashed her behind the living room sofa until Daniel got back to town 36 hours later. The image of John living with his wife's dead body behind the couch for that long was surpassed only by my discovery that at least a dozen people had passed in and out of his apartment during that time, clueless. I just shook my head. We picked up Daniel, who copped to everything, and graciously agreed to take us to Alexis's body in exchange for being let off the hook. Sorry, but we all wanted John that badly. John, however, was somewhere in California visiting his new girlfriend at that time, and nobody knew exactly where he was. We had to get Alexis's body so we could arrest him when he got back. Daniel took us straight to it, buried in the field next to the metal fabrication plant. When the forensic team found her skull only five minutes into the digging, I was suddenly awed by the fact that the grave was less than a mile from where Laurie had said to look for it, and it was indeed near water— a little creek literally touched the edge of the gravesite.

All we had to do now was nab John when he got back, but we had a small problem brewing. All of this took place during the infamous Green River killings, and somehow the media got wind of us digging up a body in a field, a body they thought was another Green River victim. We weren't allowed to confirm or deny anything to the press, so with a false story about to blast out on the airwaves, we were lucky to positively ID the body and catch John before he heard we'd found it.

John Burke was immediately charged with murder. His attorney wanted to make a deal, saying John did it under extreme emotional distress rather than with premeditation. Our district attorney suggested that if he told us all about the murder and took a polygraph to prove his story, he'd be charged with manslaughter one instead of murder. John agreed.

It turned out that 28 of the 30 things Laurie had said during our initial conversation were absolutely right on the money. John had argued with Alexis about his couch potato attitude and their money problems. She threatened divorce, and did it very loudly by screaming and stomping out the front door. When she got to her car, she realized it was cold out and she was wearing her nightgown, so she went back to the apartment, flung the door open, and started yelling again. That was her fatal mistake, more or less. John's already frayed nerves snapped, and in a fit of rage, just wanting to shut her up, he pushed her, then grabbed her throat and choked her. Alexis collapsed in a heap. Peace at last, John thought, but then he noticed that she'd urinated all over the floor. In a horrifying instant he realized she was dead.

In shock, he went into the living room, sat down, and just thought. And thought. His mind wandered, and his imagination got hold of him. Suddenly he had flashes of Stephen King–type movies, where the victim rises from the dead, grabs a sharp kitchen knife, and exacts immediate revenge. John had to make sure that didn't happen. He grabbed the heating pad he had been sitting on, went back to his wife's body, wrapped the electrical cord around her neck, then pulled good and hard. Just to make sure. Now he didn't know what the hell to do. He couldn't think without Daniel. So he hid the body behind the couch. During the next 36 hours, everyone he knows comes into the place—his family, her family—everyone. I still shake my head at that.

Daniel finally got home from the ball tournament. John told him what had happened, showed him the body, and begged him to help get rid of it. They borrowed their father's car, a large Lincoln, and loaded up the body. They also took Alexis's car and drove them both 12 miles north of Vancouver, Washington, just over the Oregon state line. They dumped Alexis's car there, in an area that looked just like what Laurie had described. Then they drove the Lincoln to the factory in the middle of the night and buried Alexis's body in the field. On a daily basis, John would go to the top of the building and look out at the gravesite, just to check on it. Imagine. And every time we rattled his cage, he was indeed running at the mouth to someone about it. But no one ever told us. John took the plea agreement and got a 20-year sentence.

A couple years ago, John decided he wanted to get things off his chest and make apologies to the people he'd lied to. So I went to the penitentiary to chat with him, and I learned that the 29th thing Laurie told me was true, too. John said that when he and Alexis used to go hiking around McMinnville, Oregon, they would spend time at a place known locally as Bell's Landing. It actually had significance for both of them. And the 30th thing? Somehow I can't even remember what that was now.

So that's how it went. The case was solved, and I'd had a psychic experience. We originally shot down a lot of what Laurie said because it had so much to do with Daniel, and we simply didn't think he could have been involved. From a cop's standpoint, I not only have to solve the case but get it into a courtroom. I can't drag a psychic along and say she told me this, she told me that. I wouldn't mind obtaining information about a case from anywhere, but the way the system is designed, I would have to take that knowledge and translate it into something acceptable to that system. Even with the insights we had, the case was solved by normal investigative procedures. But Laurie *was* terrifically accurate with everything we documented on June 3, 1986.

Do I ever consult psychics now? Well, it's not every case that you'd even want to use a psychic on, and I haven't exactly called any in, but then, I've got one of the better ones around right here in the same house.

I was so impressed with Laurie that I married her. Can you believe it? Mr. Details and Ms. I-Can-Read-Your-Mind-but-I-Can't-Find-My-Car-Keys-Again-Dear. But we've stepped a bit more into each other's very different worlds. At one time, Laurie was against guns, but now she's pretty good on the shooting range. And I've been talking to students in the classes she teaches at a local college, lecturing about using gut-level hunches at work. Am I really a believer? Well, it wasn't exactly her psychic abilities I found irresistible. I probably married her in spite of the fact that she's a psychic.

After all, she's pretty cute, too.

Ancient Medicine

The Navajo medicine woman stared into a large piece of transparent crystal and saw images: a dry river wash reaching across a northern Arizona desert expanse; clumps of cottonwood trees along the sandy banks; one small stagnant pool of water in the riverbed. She also saw a body lying facedown in the shallow pool directly under a tree, the body of a man named Blackhair. Navajo police had been searching for Blackhair in 1981, after he had wandered away from a Tuba City hospital several weeks previously. The crystal gazer saw him in her clear stone and, speaking in Navajo to the small group of police officers who sat with her, she related details of the site where Blackhair's body could be found.

Suddenly the woman's face twisted in revulsion, and she

vomited. She complained of a foul odor around the body, talking as though she was standing right next to it. "It stinks," she declared. "The man is dead."

The police officers knew she was right, and there really wasn't anything left to do now except find the site she described and retrieve the body. But the puzzle wasn't completely solved. Investigators still had to determine the *exact* location the medicine woman saw in her crystal vision. She was not able to provide anything more than what she saw, but the scene in her stone was precise about the immediate surroundings and what had happened.

Six weeks after Blackhair disappeared, his body was discovered in a spot that matched the crystal gazer's description. He was lying facedown in the water, exactly as she'd said.

When a case comes to a dead end, Navajo police occasionally turn to medicine men and women for assistance, blending ancient spiritual traditions with modern investigative techniques. Many officers, whether Native American or not, report successes using information from native spiritualists in their investigations. Spiritual practices such as crystal gazing are learned arts, the officers say, passed down from one medicine man or woman to another, a chosen few who call upon the forces of nature and the Earth to provide clues to life's problems. Their diagnostic techniques can also be used to locate crime scenes, track missing persons, and find stolen items. But, explains Raymond Barlow, an evidence technician with the Navajo police, the information generally does not reveal a perpetrator, nor does it provide precise directions to locations.

"I would say the medicine man's answers are more of a puzzle to solve than a remedy," says Barlow. "You will get a description of a site that might include landmarks, but unless you've been to that particular place before, you probably won't know exactly where it is. When police utilize a crystal gazer or other diagnostician, all they're doing is asking for more information to include in the investigation. It's just another lead. Very rarely will the answers be revealed that give you a conclusion. What you get are steps to take to come to a conclusion on your own."

In spite of that drawback, police have solved cases over the years using information from native spiritualists, everything from missing persons and thefts to murders. Many officers have a great deal of faith in the information they receive and consider it useful in helping them patrol the large, open area of the Navajo reservation in the Southwest.

The reservation is the size of a small state, stretching from Arizona's Painted Desert at its western boundary toward the Continental Divide in New Mexico at its eastern boundary, and reaching into parts of Colorado and Utah to the north. The 400-member Navajo police force has a lot of barren desert land under its jurisdiction. When investigating cases involving missing persons or stolen property, they need all the help they can get.

"The search for Blackhair covered a very large area," says Investigator Greg Adair of the Navajo Police Department of Criminal Investigations in Tuba City, Arizona. "He wandered off, and no one had a clue which direction he'd gone. All we could do was make some assumptions and start searching."

The victim had been in the hospital for a few days when he'd decided he'd had enough and just left, Adair says. He walked out in the middle of the night and presumably headed for his home about 40 miles west of the Indian Health Center in Tuba City. His family reported him missing after a day, and police began searching in an area along the dry riverbed in the direction of the victim's home.

"No one had reported seeing a man in a hospital gown along the roadway, so we figured he'd headed home through the desert," says Adair. "We searched along the most likely path he would have taken, and that was to follow the riverbed. The river usually has water in it during the winter, but this was summer so it was dry. After twice combing the area thoroughly and following the wash for about 15 miles toward Blackhair's home, we came up with nothing. So our supervisor decided to consult the crystal gazer."

Navajo women practice crystal gazing using stones gathered from one of four sacred mountains, explains Raymond Barlow. Gazers go into a trance and call upon the Earth to assist them through the crystals. They will see pictures of a particular place in the stones, mostly landmarks and distinctive rock formations within an area. "Sometimes the crystal will show them a person, but usually it's taking them to a location where something can be found or where a crime took place. The gazers provide as detailed a description of the site as possible, and hopefully enough clues will be present that police can find the place she describes."

The officers were fairly certain they had been looking for Blackhair in the right area, but the medicine woman couldn't pinpoint an exact site. After listening to her information, the searchers went back and climbed up on hilltops and ledges so they could overlook the desert floor for miles around without trying to walk the entire search pattern again. Still they found nothing, but they soon learned that the victim had done something they hadn't expected.

"Blackhair was a little mentally handicapped, a bit slow," Adair recalls. "We were correct in assuming he'd walked along the dry riverbed. But when he started home, he got confused and turned in the opposite direction, west instead of east toward his home. A sheepherder found his body six weeks after he disappeared, and he was eight miles in the wrong direction. But the location where he was found looked exactly like the spot the crystal gazer described, and the body was in the exact position she said it would be."

One member of the search team did walk about a mile the wrong way, but soon decided his efforts were fruitless. Despite the gazer's certainty that the man was along the river wash, it wasn't logical for Blackhair to have gone that way.

"We were just being a little too logical, I guess. When dealing with visions, perhaps we have to suspend logic sometimes," says Adair. "It helps when we have the manpower to go all out. If we'd had it and didn't have other cases to take care of, maybe we'd have gone further in the opposite direction. But it didn't make sense."

Adair, who is not Native American, says he has a different perspective on the use of medicine men and women than his fellow Navajo officers do.

"When the information is accurate, I sometimes try to find a different logical explanation in the back of my mind instead of just accepting it," he says. "But there isn't always another explanation. It just works sometimes, and little clues can help a lot. We were looking for some stolen turquoise jewelry once and the medicine man told us where to look for it—and we found it there."

There was a time not long ago when the Navajo Police Department actually had a fund to pay for native spiritualists to come in on certain cases, says Captain Dan Benally of Window Rock, Arizona. But with budget cutbacks in recent years, the department began to encourage family members to bring in a medicine man if they wanted to help an investigation.

"Although the information provided by a medicine man may be general, it sometimes leads us in a direction that helps solve a case, turn up evidence, or find missing items," he says.

Benally once worked on a murder case in which the victim had been decapitated. The body was located, but investigators couldn't find the head. After much searching, the department brought in a medicine man.

In this case, they brought in a hand trembler, a medicine man who searches for answers by asking the help of a common southwestern lizard, the Gila monster.

"The Gila monster feels its way around to find things," says Raymond Barlow. "The medicine man emulates the Gila monster's way of searching. First he uses prayers, herbs, and traditional medicines to ask the Gila monster for assistance. He goes into a trance, and his hand begins to tremble, to feel around for answers like the Gila monster does. He is searching, trying to find answers in the dark. The hand will draw pictures on its own in the dirt. When the trembler comes out of the trance, he will say what needs to be done in the particular situation."

In this case, the investigators simply needed to return to where they originally found the body. "The hand trembler said that the perpetrator had the head with him in another location, but that he would be bringing it back to where we found the body," Captain Benally says. "After two weeks went by, the medicine man instructed us to go back out to the site. We searched again, and this time we found the head. We had covered that area well the first time, and I know the head wasn't there. The medicine man was right. But we were unable to find the perpetrator, and the case is still unsolved."

For Native Americans, spiritualism is part of everyday life, so it's not surprising that the Navajo Police Department also turns to the old practices when they need help. The traditions have survived for centuries—and as long as belief in their effectiveness is strong, it's likely investigators will continue to search for leads using ancient medicine.

3

UFOS AND
RELATED
PHENOMENA

WHEN I WAS 10 years old, my brother and I used to make UFOS
out of plastic dry-cleaning bags, drinking straws, straight pins,
and birthday candles. Assembled properly, the homemade UFO
was essentially a hot-air balloon that could rise to some pretty
impressive heights and present great illusions of size and mass.
We'd gather all the neighborhood kids, hide behind trees, and
snicker as cars screeched to a halt and people got all excited
and called the police. The UFO was usually gone by the time
the cops arrived, so they'd just listen to the people's stories.
What could they do, anyway? Arrest the captain of the UFO
for causing a disturbance? But it was great fun, and it was all
my brother's idea, really. What did I know from UFOS?

I should have known, because in December 1965 one of the
most compelling and baffling UFO mysteries of our time happened virtually in my backyard. While we were busy bringing
traffic to a halt on Route 160 in southwestern Pennsylvania,
an uninvited visitor fell from the sky and crashed into the
woods near the small town of Kecksburg, less than 40 miles
west of our home. This one wasn't a hot-air balloon. Volun-
teer firefighters and local police thought a small plane had gone
down. But before they actually found the wreckage, military

A replica of a UFO that crashed in Kecksburg, Pennsylvania, in 1965 sits atop the town fire hall. (COURTESY OF STAN GORDON, RESEARCHER, GREENSBURG, PA)

personnel mysteriously appeared, took control of the scene, and ordered the state police to block off access to the site. As the night wore on, only military vehicles were admitted, including a large, empty flatbed truck. That truck later emerged from the forest with a full military escort, and it carried a large bell-shaped object hidden under a tarp. Officially the cargo was a meteorite, but a few people who did manage to see the object before troops arrived say it was a copper-bronze colored craft with bizarre markings on it that resembled Egyptian hieroglyphics. Today a replica of that UFO, constructed according to eyewitness descriptions, sits in a place of honor atop Kecksburg's fire hall, a curious monument to a bizarre event that to this day is unexplained.

No wonder all those people on Route 160 were so upset.

Real or Imagined?

The United States government says the UFO phenomenon is not real, a position it has maintained for nearly 50 years. That position is based on the results—or lack of results—of its own UFO studies, most notably Project Blue Book, which was closed in 1969. The studies concluded that most UFOs could be explained as natural or man-made phenomena. The fact that researchers were unable to find explanations for a large number of the sightings seems to have been ignored. Currently, there are no known government UFO studies in progress, though sightings over military installations are still investigated.

We are supposed to believe that tens of thousands of people who have seen UFOs over the past several decades didn't really see anything, or that what they saw was explainable in some way. There have even been theories suggesting that a mass psychosis is responsible for sightings and abduction accounts. But the bottom line is this: there is no physical evidence whatsoever for the existence of UFOs.

So what about the Kecksburg object and the Roswell, New Mexico, disk, and others like them that are allegedly secreted away at various military bases across the country? What about photographs, crash debris, and former government officials who tend to verify what it seems people want to believe?

There has been a proliferation of independent UFO investigators and organizations who are determined to answer just those questions. Today it's increasingly difficult to separate the wheat from the chaff in this highly controversial field. The vast array of popular theories ranges from the sublime to the ridiculous, with aliens both benevolent and aggressive playing a major role in various scenarios. Quite often, so does the U.S. government (read: military), which is either working with the aliens toward some mysterious goal—or they're not. The government knows why the visitors are here—or they don't. We have captured some of the creatures—or we haven't. It's a nonstop guessing game, and no one knows who or what to believe.

Some speculators hold that the aliens in UFOs are actually human time travelers from Earth's future who have some urgent reason for returning to the past. Perhaps they are in need of something they no longer have but we still do. Or they are trying to prevent some catastrophe from befalling them in the future by stopping the precipitating factors in our time period. I personally find this theory intriguing and palatable, partially because it suggests that we ourselves are the aliens— or at least their ancestors.

But UFOS also are explained away as weather balloons, swamp gas, plasma phenomena, commercial jetliners, meteors/ meteorites, stars, the moon, optical illusions, hallucinations, mass hysteria, and just about any other thing you can think of. So many theories—what's a poor earthling to do? It's been 50 years since the first widely reported UFO sighting, and we still don't *know* anything. However, it's rumored that we will soon find out. As the end of the millennium nears, word is spreading rapidly that our government will confess to the whole cover-up. Or will it?

"Not likely. Everyone thinks it will be any day now, but that talk has been going through the UFO communities for over 40 years, and it still hasn't happened," says Larry Fawcett, a 30-year law enforcement veteran and noted UFO researcher. In the 1970s, the now-retired lieutenant from the Coventry Police Department in Connecticut took up the cause of prying UFO information out of the government via the Federal Freedom of Information Act. He has chronicled the results of his groundbreaking campaign in his book, *The UFO Cover-Up*.

From the beginning, Fawcett has looked at the UFO phenomenon from the investigative perspective of a police officer who has himself experienced a sighting that had a profound impact on his life. What bothers him most about the whole UFO puzzle is the complete lack of physical evidence to prove their existence.

"We're dealing with something that so far has turned up no physical evidence. How can there be no evidence for something that's gone on for decades? This is where we get into the *very* high strangeness of all this," he says.

"I've talked with many people who report having seen UFOS, and they're very sincere in what they say. But the one thing that's going to get the government to acknowledge what's going on is to come up with a piece of a UFO or be able to say, 'Here's an alien.' There has to be something solid."

But some people claim they *do* have such solid evidence. Alleged pieces of crashed disks from Roswell and other sites aren't making anyone in authority talk, however. The popular government line is that those people are lying, proved by the fact that the composition of those items contain elements known here on Earth. The government plays on that idea, says Fawcett, even though rocks brought back from the moon also contain earthly mineral components such as gold, silver, copper, and nickel.

"What should raise eyebrows is when these items are found to contain a purity of 100 percent, something that we can't do within our science," he says.

The reason that many say we won't learn the truth about UFOs soon lies in a popular belief that many of the unknown craft sighted are military in nature. The government deals in weapons delivery systems, says Fawcett, and that has been the key to all the secrecy since the 1950s. "In the military theories, UFOs are (a) created from the ground up by our own government, or (b) they are created by our government using highly advanced technology from crashed alien craft, or (c) they are completely alien craft actually being flown by our military," he says. "Which one it is or why, we don't know."

It can boggle the mind to consider the possibilities of this phenomenon and the reasons why our government and military might be involved. But secrecy is one thing the military is very good at, so we may wait a long time for any official explanations.

Cops and UFOs

The course and history of the UFO phenomena have been marked by considerable changes in both ideas and attitudes. If a serious researcher were to stand up today and announce that, based on all his years of experience, he knows what UFOs are, society would likely take the news with sincere interest and far less ridicule than it would have 20 or 30 years ago. Well-known people in politics, entertainment, and the sciences have publicly admitted to sighting UFOs, as have a handful of former NASA astronauts. When sightings now occur, people often report them to police, whereas previously they would have remained silent. It's almost trendy to witness a UFO at this point, and the public is less apt to immediately label sighters as crackpots. So why does it still seem to be a big deal if a police officer reports a sighting?

The officer's own department usually has a major problem with such reports. Larry Fawcett says that when he was a cop, he actually cared little about what the public or his department thought about him and his UFO-related activities. Everyone knew he had experienced a sighting before he became a cop, that he wrote books on the topic, that he had legally faced off with the government, and that he was committed to investigating the phenomenon.

"I never suffered ridicule from my colleagues because I was very outspoken about what I was doing," he says. "And I really didn't care what they thought because they didn't lay out the money to sue the government—I did. Once we began to get the information and learned more about what was going on, everyone's opinion of the phenomenon changed quite a bit. Every now and then I'd get a joke, but it was all in fun."

Based on personal experience and decades of research, Fawcett asserts that a large number of police officers experience UFO sightings. But they don't report them, mostly due to an unspoken rule in many departments that says simply *keep quiet*. What is the source of this stance? It might be based on the former military experience of many police officers. Those who served in the military may have had sightings of various unidentified objects during that time. If they reported the sightings, they were dealt with in one of three ways.

"They were usually told not to speak of the occurrence. Or a group of people might be transferred out to different bases so they couldn't talk among themselves about the issue," says Fawcett. "Or a report was filed, and they never heard another word about it."

Ridicule and the threat to one's career are more reasons for keeping quiet. It's popularly believed that years ago ridicule was the government's unofficial way of dispensing with UFO sightings. Perhaps police and fire departments clammed up as a result of that. Or there may be established policies that say, "Don't report it. We don't want to hear it, or your career is ruined." Still, Fawcett finds it puzzling that many police departments react this way. "Perhaps they simply feel the public wouldn't be comfortable with their cops seeing UFOs," he says.

Some cops say they would come forward anyway *if* they were to spot a UFO. One state police officer told me that he would file a report if he saw a UFO because he feels it's the right thing to do. He has little fear of what might happen to him regarding his career, but confessed that he can afford to take that stand, unlike many cops. The specters of termination or being passed over for promotions are very real. But this cop says there would be—at least for him—a great internal need to be forthcoming about such an outré experience that would eclipse any potential threat to his career. If he felt that strongly about it, then why wouldn't he let me quote him by name?

"I would cross that UFO bridge only if I actually came to it," he stated.

He hits on a valid point, though. The analytical cop who wants to solve every puzzle he or she comes across could really have a tough time with a UFO sighting. It defies explanation, and for a cop, that's not good. Several officers who have had sightings and spoke with me on condition of anonymity have expressed distress at not being able to share their experiences openly. Some exert a tremendous effort to put the experience behind them, while others gravitate toward organizations such as the Mutual UFO Network (MUFON) to find kindred spirits. Except for their jobs, these cops are just like anyone else who might stumble upon the unknown. They feel a need to talk about the experience, particularly with others who have been in similar situations. I find it unfortunate that they can't speak openly, since the detailed accounts of these trained observers could be very useful in ongoing research.

The experiences aren't just limited to seeing flying craft, either. Other phenomena associated with UFOs can be equally disturbing.

Cattle Mutilations

One of the strangest and most persistent phenomena associated with UFOs is unexplained animal mutilations, most often occurring with cattle. Mutilations have been reported in all parts of the world since at least the 1960s and generally in areas where frequent UFO sightings were reported. Descriptions of the mutilations are strikingly consistent: Incisions are done with a "surgical precision"; the animal's sexual organs are removed; the anus is cored out; strips of skin are sliced from the face and jaw areas; and all of these operations produce no bleeding. Carcasses often contain inordinate levels of radiation, and an odor resembling that of battery acid sometimes emanates from the animal's mouth. These mutilations have baffled law enforcement agencies for decades. Officials have yet to determine who is doing them, how they're done, and why.

Everyone from government investigators to college professors to private researchers and ranchers has a theory. The list of possible culprits is a real grab bag, including, but not limited to, extraterrestrial aliens; chemical-biological warfare experiments; disease; gang rituals; hitchhikers; satanic cults; oil companies; lightning; hungry homeless people; secret military experiments (possibly conducted jointly with aliens); and natural predators such as coyotes.

Which theories make more sense than others is debatable.

If it's a disease, it would have to be a very strange one to leave such bizarre, specific damage to a cow's body. Gangs and cults? Not unless they're carrying around some awfully expensive lasers. The mutilations are too clean and precise, which also rules out lightning, the homeless, and, we assume, hitchhikers. The government is always a good bet in such secretive matters. But if federal researchers want cattle so badly for experimentation, why not just raise their own herds instead of raising people's suspicions? Likewise for oil companies. As for aliens, few people could even begin to guess what use they might have in mind for cattle parts.

At the present, it seems we're not even close to finding the answer.

"No perpetrators have ever been caught by law enforcement in 20 years. No one can back up claims that this is being done by satanic cults, the government, or whoever," says Larry Fawcett. "Cults are a popular argument, but if that's the case, the intelligence community certainly would have turned up the perpetrators doing it. This hasn't happened, and people are completely baffled."

The problem became so massive in the American Southwest in the 1970s that law enforcement demanded help from state and federal government agencies. This was serious business to ranchers, who were suffering financial hardship from loss of livestock often worth up to $1,000 a head. In 1980, what was supposed to be the definitive study was brought about by Senator Harrison Schmidt of New Mexico and conducted by Ken Rommel, Jr., a former FBI agent. Rommel's findings, which concluded that natural predators were to blame, were consistent with many other official investigations. The only other thing that was constant in the whole situation was how infuriated law enforcement agencies became each time a study arrived at that conclusion. They considered the "natural predators" explanation to be beyond inadequate and an insult to their intelligence.

"That was a big whitewash. The government wanted in

some way to hush up the mutilations, and they tried to do that using Rommel," Fawcett states. "The sheriffs who investigated these cases knew it wasn't predators because they know what predatory mutilation looks like. Most of them were ranchers themselves and had been around livestock all their lives."

Comparing the facts of the mutilations with how natural predators would bring down a cow does indeed present some glaring differences. A coyote or cougar would knock the cow's legs out from under it and drop it to the ground, producing scratch marks on the animal's rear end and elsewhere. Next the predator would suffocate the cow by seizing it by the throat to cut off the windpipe. Was anything like this seen? "There's no evidence of this type of predatory kill in these cases—none whatsoever," says Fawcett.

The cattle mutilation debate rages on. Police still investigate mutilations as destruction of property cases while ranchers continue to endure more financial losses—and the trail of dead animals leads nowhere.

Crop Circles

Talk about strange—someone, somehow, is getting a real kick out of leaving large perfect circles and intricate patterns in the world's corn and wheat fields. The impressions appear out of nowhere and can be a few feet across or as large as 500 feet in diameter. The term *agriglyph* has been adopted, but is really not accurate anymore since the phenomenon also has been found in snow, mud, and sand. Theories on how these patterns are made range from military radio waves, plasma vortexes, and tornadoes to—you guessed it—UFOs. And let's not slight that most insidious of all suspected perpetrators, the hoaxster.

It's pretty much believed that agriglyphs are hoaxes. But if that's true, it would mean that several centuries worth of pranksters had little else to do than trample some farmer's crops in the middle of the night. To me, that would be a far more mind-boggling phenomenon than the circles themselves.

The first reported agriglyphs date back to 1678 in England.
That's plenty of time to catch an international conspiracy of
farm vandals red-handed. But it's not been done. While two
men in England claimed responsibility for 200 English crop
circles in 1991, there have been many thousands of such patterns all over the world still unaccounted for.

The circles are not dangerous and are curiosities at best.
Researchers are still trying to determine exactly how, and why
the patterns are made, and by whom. When new circles are
found, police usually are called. They look at the patterns,
maybe take some photos, then turn to dealing with the crowds
of people often attracted to the site. After the furor dies down,
the circles are generally forgotten.

The UFO theory seems to stick better than others, so it's
always interesting to note how much UFO activity is reported
in an area during the time crop circles are found. Often there
is plenty. One has to wonder about the possible connection.
Beyond that, there's not much else to do except hope that someday someone will actually witness a crop circle being made.

Government Cover-Ups

I have to touch on this subject because I may or may not have
run into a government cover-up myself, and I find it intriguing that authorities could deny an event witnessed by hundreds
of people. But I heard it myself when I tried to get information on an alleged UFO crash that occurred on Long Island on
November 24, 1992.

On that date, an object blazed through the night sky and
plummeted into a remote area of Southaven Park in the town
of Shirley. Some of my friends who live near the area vividly
recall the incident because traffic on the Long Island Express-
way was backed up for miles and local television news ran several reports on the strange crash. Supposedly the local fire
district and Suffolk County Police responded to the crash scene.
But it's said they were met there by the fire brigade from nearby

Brookhaven National Laboratory and several stereotypical unmarked federal cars driven by unmarked federal men. The locals were told to move along as the feds took control of the whole situation. Access to Southaven Park was closed for nearly a week, something local residents say is extremely out of the ordinary. When questioned, park officials claimed the park was closed for duck hunting. Depending on who was asked, however, some claimed that it never really closed at all.

Journalists and UFO investigators looked into the matter and were unable to find anyone in authority who would acknowledge that anything at all happened that night. It was quite curious because so many people had seen the fireball and the fire rescue activity. A few local residents claimed to have actually seen a crashed spacecraft in the park. Even more residents on the park's perimeter came forward to say they experienced bizarre incidents in their homes such as phones going dead and the sudden failure of battery-operated items. I called the police and the fire district to ask about their opinion of the whole incident, and was told that no calls of any kind had come into their stations the night of the incident. The fire department claimed their equipment and men never left the station house that night. I found this response fascinating.

I suppose if the interests of national security were involved, a cover-up could be pulled off. But what do the conversations sound like when local police and fire departments are told what to do in this instance by a higher authority? I can only imagine. But I sure am curious to know, officially or unofficially, what really happened in Southaven Park on the night of November 24, 1992. Unfortunately, says Larry Fawcett, we can't hold our collective breath waiting for official versions of such incidents.

"All UFO-related incidents go to the Pentagon to an office that handles them. But very few people really know the whole picture," he says. "Some people know bits and pieces because of their particular jobs, but no one other than a select few knows the whole story. It's going to be very difficult to ever get the whole truth until the Powers That Be decide that we're going to get the whole truth."

There are police officers who *will* talk about their experiences in this area, and I found a few. It's safe to say that all of their lives were changed. "Encounter" tells of a Florida deputy who detailed his frightening UFO sighting in an official police report and how that action may have cost him his job. In another story, a retired sheriff from Illinois hung on to his position by keeping quiet about his remarkable sighting nearly 30 years ago. But the discovery of crop circles in his area in 1992 brought him forward to tell his story in "Invasion of the Corn Stompers." In 1993, in a neighboring state, two helicopter patrolmen encountered a strange object that from its description looked a lot like my famous dry-cleaning bag UFO. But in "Chase," we find that this UFO did things no cleaning bag—or anything else I can think of—could possibly have done. Lastly, a strange story of cattle mutilations from New Mexico and Colorado is told in "An Incident in Mora County."

Encounter

Florida had barely recovered from Hurricane Andrew's destruction when eight months later in April 1993 a fierce windstorm struck in the west-central part of the state. The powerful storm the locals called the "Storm of the Century" produced hurricane-type damage in Hernando County, about 40 miles north of Tampa on the coast. Special police patrols were sent out to tend to emergencies, provide security, and assist anyone who needed help. On the night of Friday, April 16, in an area called Pine Island, one Hernando County sheriff's deputy experienced something that changed his life forever.

Ron Chancey had 21 years in law enforcement at the time, having previously worked for the Florida Highway Patrol, the

Hillsborough County Sheriff's Office (Tampa), and the Dade City Police. He had been with the Hernando County Sheriff's Office for a little over a month when he was assigned to patrol the Pine Island area on the 8:00 P.M. to 8:00 A.M. shift. After the onslaught of the storm, Pine Island was a mess. Houses were flooded or blown apart from high winds, vehicles had been swept away as streets became raging rivers, trees and power lines were down, and sand dunes covered many road-ways. Access to these areas was closed, and residents of the Pine Island peninsula were evacuated except for a few hearty souls who chose to remain in their homes. The night was dark but clear and beautiful. As Chancey drove through Bayport, he noticed a group of people enjoying the evening at a park.

The deputy continued on the five-mile trip to Pine Island, drove to where the road dead-ended at the beach, then started back toward Bayport to the east. The road was deserted, and Chancey poked along at about 25 miles per hour, with the windows rolled down, taking in the scenery. He glanced out the driver's window toward the sky, noticed some bluish-colored lights, and turned his attention back to the road. Suddenly something dawned on him.

"It was just one of those things—those lights had looked like the Crystal River nuclear power plant up the coast. It just loomed up in the horizon. But I thought it couldn't have been the power plant. That's 50 miles north, and I'd never seen it that clearly even when I was up close to it," says Chancey. "I drove a bit further along and looked again, and the lights were paralleling me! It clicked at that point that something was wrong with this picture. That thing was moving along with me."

Awestruck, Chancey was now aware of a huge, dark boomerang-shaped object flying about 300 feet above the ground beside him. Neon-blue lights shone from the bottom of the craft. It didn't make a sound.

Chancey thought, *Well, I guess there's something wrong with me. I can't be seeing something out here because there's nothing here, only the people on the island. I'm seeing things.*

He chuckled uneasily at his own denial and kept driving along, thinking, *I didn't see this.* Purposely not looking out his side window, he drove another mile or so, then couldn't resist looking again. The black boomerang was still moving along with him. Scared but curious, Chancey stopped the car in the middle of the road, got out, and shone his spotlight on the flying machine. It had stopped, too.

"I got no reflection back because the thing was flat black in color, totally nonreflective. It looked to be about 200 to 300 feet in length from tip to tip. The only thing I could think it might be, despite its size, was a Harrier jet, which can hover. But they make an awful noise, and this was completely silent," Chancey recalls. "To be sure, I turned off the car engine and temporarily shut off my radios which, now that I think about it, is scary because I was out of communication at that point. But I still couldn't hear anything, not a thing."

Chancey studied the object for a few minutes as it silently hovered. It had no markings of any kind, no details other than the small, brilliant blue lights. Suddenly panic shot through him, and he thought, *Ron, it's time to go!* He jumped back into his patrol car, turned on all the radios and—with nothing but straight deserted road ahead of him—put the car into the wind. "I was going probably 90 to 100 miles per hour and guess what—it was running right with me again. I just kept thinking, *Get out of here. Get out of here.* My thought was that if this is something extraordinary, so to speak, I was really concerned about what might happen next. I'd never in my life considered being abducted by anything like that. Hell, I realized I'd never even thought about UFOs before. To me, the subject was sort of like a loaf of bread—it's just there. UFOs are just part of our culture, and I'd never concerned myself with it. But this . . . this was different."

The road now had sharp turns in it, but Chancey kept going as fast as he could. The black wing followed his lead, banking through the turns with him. Hoping to make it go away, Chancey reached out the window and aimed the spotlight on his pursuer once more, but now it broke rank. The thing turned at a nearly impossible angle, cut across the road in front of Chancey's car, and shot toward Bayport at an unreal speed.

"It was out of sight in a flash. The way it swooped and cut across the road was almost as if it was thumbing its nose at me," he says.

As it blitzed away, Chancey saw an amber-colored light at the craft's rear. It was not a flame like an F-14 would make, he says, but was more like looking straight into a flashlight, a very powerful light. "I was relieved that it was gone, but at the same time I was wondering what the heck had just happened. I thought maybe I was having a dream."

With the skies clear and dark again, Chancey pulled his patrol unit to the side of the road near an empty, darkened restaurant. As he took time to compose himself, he realized that if the object was flying back toward Bayport, the people at the park would *have* to see it. He sped back to Bayport on the still-deserted road.

The little park, complete with picnic tables and fishing pier, was a great place for families to sit and watch the sunset over the Gulf of Mexico. The few people Chancey saw earlier were still there, but one vehicle was starting to leave the parking lot. Chancey flipped on his blue lights and stopped the car, not quite sure if he was hoping others had seen the object or not. A teenage couple in the first car wondered what was going on.

"I didn't want to let them know what I'd seen; I wanted them to tell me what *they'd* seen, if anything. I chit-chatted for a bit, then I asked if they'd seen anything unusual. They hesitated, then said no," Chancey recalls. "I changed my tune a bit and told them what I was really trying to do was pick their minds because, if they'd been there that long, they probably *had* seen something unusual. I said, 'I can't tell you what it is, but I want *you* to tell me the truth. Be truthful with me because I'm trying to convince myself that I'm not crazy.'"

The young couple looked at each other, hesitated again,

then reluctantly admitted that they had seen something. They described the same boomerang-shaped object, right down to the blue neon lights and its flashy, grand exit. Chancey stopped the next car—same questions, same answers. Everyone else had seen the UFO. Now Chancey had a decision to make.

"I knew a group of our deputies was nearby. I thought about it for a few minutes, then I went to see them," he said. "I asked if they'd seen anything. They laughed at me, and that right there discouraged me. They took a weird attitude, too. One of them said, 'Well, I don't think I have, but if I did, I don't really care.' I honestly believe they saw the thing. If they were out there and if they were paying attention at all, I know they would have seen it. That's what we get paid to do—observe."

One of the deputies even ventured to say that what everyone *probably* saw was a local fellow flying around in his home-built ultralight. An ultralight that can hover and has the same lighting configuration as a nuclear power plant? "I don't think so," Chancey says dryly. "But that was his excuse."

Still concerned, Chancey decided to consult his lieutenant. Not wanting to talk about his encounter on the police radio, he phoned the lieutenant instead and related what had happened. The lieutenant believed him, Chancey thought.

"What should I do?" he asked his superior. "Should I forget about it, or file a report?"

The lieutenant chuckled. "Write a report," he replied, "because if you don't, you'll surely get into a jam."

Chancey slowly hung up the phone. "I knew I was dead at that point—people would think I was crazy. He wanted the report to make sure we had ourselves covered. I was damned if I did and damned if I didn't. But I felt better writing it, because that way it's in black and white." It was near dawn on Saturday when Chancey wrote the report. On Monday, his day off, Chancey went to the station early to file it, then went home.

Each day, members of the local press come into the sheriff's office to read through new reports. By noon, everyone had read the UFO saga, and all hell broke loose. Chancey was asked to come into the station to face a media mob of local television stations and newspapers who wanted to hear all about it. From that point on, Chancey did little but field press interviews, which soon came in from all over the country. It didn't take long for the general citizenry to start calling with their two cents as well.

"I heard from a lot of crackpots, but I also got calls from a lot of real people who said they'd seen the same thing. Some were glory freaks, I'm sure, but I feel some were very honest about it," Chancey says. Two people struck him in particular. An Orlando astronomer said he'd seen the object while stargazing through his telescope that Friday night. It flew through his frame like a blast of light, zooming across the sky in no time. He passed along the phone number of an Orange County sheriff's deputy who had also seen it, warning that the officer probably wouldn't admit to that. Chancey called anyway. "He wasn't rude to me, but he was scared," says Chancey. "He said he really didn't want to get into it."

A Miami Metro Dade police sergeant also phoned with information from a British newspaper about the U.S. military's alleged top secret project Aurora, the newest version of the Stealth aircraft. Supposedly, the chevron-shaped Aurora has the ability to hover at low altitude and fly extraordinarily fast. Chancey, an aircraft buff, doubts that's what he saw. "I personally can't fathom anybody coming up with a jet that can get to that speed in that short a distance. Besides, I don't believe the military would be flying their stuff around where people can see it. They would test fly at an altitude where we'd never see it, and they certainly wouldn't be flying low, kind of taunting you with it."

Indeed, Chancey had already checked with nearby McDill Air Force Base, where an air show was staged that same weekend, and with another military outfit in Pensacola. Both denied having anything out flying that night.

As the weeks and months passed, Chancey got tired of the crackpots and of the snickering from his fellow officers. He even lost interest in following up some good leads on the military angle. Making matters worse, all this occurred while he was embroiled in some problems in his personal life. Then came the final blow—in October 1993, Chancey was terminated from the Hernando County Sheriff's Office. The reason cited: not performing to standards. Chancey doesn't buy it.

"I was in a six-month, new-hire probationary period when the sighting occurred, during which time the department could fire at will. In a way, I wasn't in the least bit surprised," he says. "At the time, a public information officer unofficially told a reporter, whom I knew, that I was probably crazy or something. He said that he didn't believe in UFOs—which really has no bearing on it, what he believes or doesn't believe. But it got back to me, and I can see where they're coming from. They have a tight little ship and don't like to make waves." When contacted in early 1996, the Hernando County Sheriff's Office denied the termination had anything to do with the UFO sighting.

Though it bothered him at first, Chancey didn't contest the termination. Disenchanted, he looked back on a 21-year-long career in law enforcement and decided he would simply retire. By this time, the endless calls from reporters and "truth seekers" had died down. Despite losing his employment, life had settled down again.

He still wonders about what he saw, and wonders how different things might have been had he kept his mouth shut. Officially, the sheriff's office had never told him not to talk to the press. Unofficially, they probably would have been happier if he hadn't.

Would he do it again? "No way. Looking back, I never should have said anything about it, let alone filed a report. But keeping all that inside, I'm sure, would have had a very negative effect on me," Chancey says. "I know what I saw. It's changed my life forever and got me thinking about my beliefs. I really have to believe that there is something else out there. And as wonderful as that prospect can be, it's also somewhat scary."

Ron Chancey doesn't want to think that we are the only intelligent species in this entire universe. If this right here is the amount of our intelligence, he says, then there's something sadly missing overall. He often wonders what the odds are of one solo cop on a lonely road late at night seeing something this extraordinary. Considering the potential consequences of admitting to such an experience, perhaps the odds aren't as great as he might think.

Rock Island County sheriff's deputies investigate Ed Lawson's crop circle. (COURTESY OF ROCK ISLAND COUNTY SHERIFF'S OFFICE— SHERIFF MIKE GRCHAN)

Invasion of the Corn Stompers

The *Chicago Tribune* called it a UFO—an "Unidentified Farm Object." Ed Lawson and his wife were amazed at the hordes of people who made a pilgrimage to their northwestern Illinois farm to see it and touch it. Where it came from and when it arrived were uncertain; who or what was involved in creating it was unclear. The only thing that was *perfectly* clear was the absolutely perfect 46^1/$_2$-foot circle of swirled, flattened cornstalks that Lawson found in one of his fields on October 16, 1990. There in rural Rock Island County, the sheriff's office had to take on the rare duty of crowd control as word got out about the first reported crop circle in this vast farming area. A constant parade of humanity descended on Lawson's little green acres like Woodstock hippies to Max Yasgar's farm. Newspaper and television reporters, believers and nonbelievers, seers and sightseers, experts and the merely curious—even an alleged "government man"—flocked to the scene in the days following Ed Lawson's discovery. They all wanted to see the strange circle and, perhaps, to catch a glimpse of who or what made it.

While folks twittered about UFOs leaving an otherworldly impression in the cornfield, Sheriff Mike Grchan was pretty sure that earthbound human children were responsible. But no one—human or extraterrestrial—ever came forward to take credit for causing the whole uproar. Grchan's investigators simply couldn't explain what made the crop circle or how it was done.

If studied closely, the circle itself was impressive. Nine-foot cornstalks were broken down and flattened to the ground, swirled neatly in a clockwise direction. The circle appeared to have been stamped right out of the middle of the field, with no paths leading to it from any direction. Corn cobs were embedded as deep as five inches into the hard-packed earth, which was baffling, since it would have required a tremendous weight to accomplish that feat. There were a few footprints under the stalks, but Ed Lawson said he himself might have made them when he first found the circle. He also noted that perhaps the many visitors had left the prints.

Though the strange dent in the field caused a lot of commotion for several days, most local residents simply ignored the fuss. A few people couldn't ignore it, however, and those folks were moved to tell Ed Lawson a few secrets, some of them many years old. It seems this quiet area of the heartland has had its share of mysterious events over the decades, including several UFO sightings during that year. In fact, a woman had spotted a disklike flyer rising out of the woods only a few days before the circle was found. Coincidentally or not, she lived close by Ed Lawson's farm. A man also reported that a UFO made his car stop dead in its tracks, but when he took the car to the mechanic, there was nothing wrong with it. And four teenagers leaving a drive-in movie one night noticed a strange light hovering in the sky. When they drove closer, they found it to be a huge, oddly shaped craft that they chased for several miles.

Most intriguing of all, however, was the story Ed Lawson heard from an old school friend. Josiah Lemon, the retired sheriff of neighboring Mercer County, showed up at the farm to advise Ed not to take his crop circle lightly. Seeing the circle and its size had brought back a flood of memories, he told Lawson, because the diameter of the circle was almost the exact size of an elusive UFO that Lemon and other police officers had chased for an entire night in 1968.

Sheriff Josiah "Joe" Lemon (retired)
(COURTESY OF JOE LEMON)

Lemon and three friends were sitting at the sheriff's office one Sunday night, just shooting the breeze, when they heard chatter on the police radio about a strange object in the sky in Knox County, just to the east of Mercer County. Their curiosity piqued, the four men jumped into the car and drove 10 miles to the county line in hopes of catching a glimpse of the UFO. It was 9:00 P.M. in early October. The sky was dark, clear, and moonless. Lemon parked the car on the roadside where they could see for miles across flat farmland. Everything was silent for a short time. Then suddenly they heard a bizarre whirring noise coming toward them that sounded like a huge toy top spinning.

The men saw nothing across the fields, but the grating noise was deafeningly close by. They leaped out of the car and were astonished to see a large disk hovering a few hundred feet in the sky directly above them.

"It was charcoal colored and didn't have any markings on it," Lemon recalls. "The disk was flat on top, about 50 feet in diameter, and was surrounded by a halo of bright light. The light made it look like a huge glowing ball."

The UFO remained suspended in one place for a few minutes, then it moved away and vanished. But it didn't fly away at rapid speed.

"It popped out of sight, like when you turn off a light-bulb," Lemon says. "It just disappeared into thin air."

Stunned, the four men could hardly believe their eyes. They composed themselves for a few minutes, then began driving back to the sheriff's office. Lemon scanned the night sky as he drove along, and then blinked in surprise when the flying disk suddenly popped back into view directly ahead of him. He slammed on the brakes. The UFO flew off into the distance, where it frolicked and floated over open fields, like a gigantic shining beach ball bouncing, for nearly 10 minutes. Lemon grabbed the CB radio microphone and quickly alerted the sheriff of Henderson County to the southwest, telling him to go outside to see the UFO. But after a few moments, the disk vanished again.

"We were absolutely stumped," says Lemon, "We got halfway back to the office when we saw the dang thing once more. We watched it fly around for another 10 minutes, and again, just like turning a light off, it was gone."

Soon, police officers from several towns were jamming the CB radio with their own sightings of the UFO. It moved from town to town, and Lemon followed it. Other patrol units began to tag along with him, creating a caravan of cops that chased the glowing disk through several jurisdictions. All night long, the UFO popped in and out of view, almost as though it was purposely taking everyone on a merry chase. As the skies became tinted with the early light of dawn, the UFO didn't reappear as often. Finally, at daybreak, it disappeared for the last time, leaving behind a score of baffled police officers.

Exhausted, Lemon went back to his office to find news reporters and citizens demanding to know what the strange object was. One man told him he and his wife had been out driving the night before when the disk appeared and flew alongside them. His wife had become completely hysterical, he said. Lemon also learned that many people's television sets had been on the blink since the night before, including his chief deputy's. The TVs sputtered with static, flashing on and off for most of the night. The only thing Lemon could tell people for sure was that the object wasn't an airplane, but he had no idea what it was. He cautiously downplayed the event in public. Eventually, most people shrugged off the whole incident.

"People think you're nuts if you talk about seeing something like that. I just hushed up about it and that was it," he says. "But I've done a terrible lot of thinking since then. That object certainly wasn't a man-made thing from around here, and it definitely wasn't a joke. People might think that I'm crazy, but I know what I saw, and no one can ever take that away from me."

For the longest time afterward, Lemon couldn't stop himself from frequently glancing up at the sky. He kept thinking he'd see the UFO again one day but never has. Back in 1968, he didn't hear any reports of crop circles being found in the area. But then, he speculates that people wouldn't have had a clue about such things and certainly wouldn't have thought to report a circle to the police even if they *had* found one. Besides, in a peaceful little corner of the world like Rock Island County, Illinois, it's difficult to imagine such strange events cropping up, so to speak.

Just who the "corn stompers" were may never be known. What *is* known is that Josiah Lemon had a remarkable experience that he'll never forget. It is also known that Sheriff Grchan still wouldn't mind hearing from the pranksters he thinks somehow managed the difficult task of turning agriculture into artwork. And it's a pretty good bet that Ed Lawson wishes he'd never found that perfect circle stamped out of his cornfield in the first place.

Chase

The world looks different from a helicopter. Just like on a map, the streets below appear as perfect squares and rectangles, and homes are set in perfectly straight, neat rows. Knowing how to read that three-dimensional map is an art learned by police air patrol officers, particularly the observer, who watches the ground while his partner flies the chopper. The observer can recognize landmarks, judge distances, adjust for speed and depth perception, and identify a scurrying ant as a fleeing burglary suspect. This all sounded very interesting to Patrol Officer Kenny Downs of the Jefferson County Police Department in Louisville, Kentucky. Downs was asked to fill in for an observer who was away on medical leave. He thought it might be fun, something different, to be above the streets instead of on them. Downs was partnered with Patrol Officer Kenny Graham, a veteran chopper pilot known for his flying skills and attention to safety issues, which made Downs feel comfortable. Helicopters are odd birds, so to speak, and it's best to be with a pilot who really knows his stuff.

The partners were on routine air patrol the night of February 28, 1993, not long after Downs's temporary assignment began. It was a crisp and cold Friday evening just after a snowfall, which had left a couple feet of fresh white stuff on the ground. But the skies were clear and visibility seemed endless in spite of the dark. Just before midnight, after flying for nearly an hour, pilot Graham started back to the heliport when a call on the radio caught his attention. A possible home break-in was occurring near the city's large General Electric plant. Since they were close to the scene, Graham banked the chopper around to lend support to the ground patrol units. It took only a few minutes before they saw the familiar open fields and huge, empty parking lots of the factory, blanketed with untouched new snow. With no sign of the patrol cars as yet, the chopper hovered to wait. Both officers scanned the scene below for anything unusual.

Almost instantly, Graham spotted a strange light in the treetops by the factory, a bright orange glow that was too large to be a streetlight. He pointed it out to Downs, who looked puzzled.

"You think it's a tower? A light on top of an antenna?" he asked.

Graham studied the strange gleaming light. "No, no, it's not. I don't think that's a tower."

Dropping a bit in altitude, Graham began a wide circle around the light. At first he thought it might have been a freak reflection off the chopper's bubble, but as he flew around the brilliant orange ball, it suddenly began to move. From the chopper, the motion was barely perceptible. The light drifted slowly a few feet back and forth, then stopped. As Graham took the chopper back up to normal flight altitude—about 500 feet—Downs turned on the spotlight and pointed it at the object. Suddenly the orange ball rose rapidly to the same altitude. Whatever it was it hovered on Downs's side of the chopper, and he got a good look at it.

The object was pear-shaped, about four to six feet in height and three feet in diameter. It seemed to be made up of two distinct parts. The overall object looked like a transparent casing, like heavy glass an inch or two thick but oddly fragile looking. Inside the casing sat the basketball-sized glowing orange light. It wasn't blindingly bright, but certainly strong enough to see for a great distance. Before Downs had the chance to form an opinion, the object suddenly zoomed straight up and out of sight.

"*What* the . . . ?!" Downs blinked in amazement. As Graham moved the chopper forward, the object suddenly dropped back down in front of them as quickly as it had disappeared. The flying pear now swung in a wide arc around the chopper. As fragile as it appeared, it moved with ease against the helicopter's rotor wash, definitely propelled by its own power. Graham's full attention was on flying the chopper. He didn't see what the object was doing until he heard Downs's excited voice in his headphones.

"Kenny, it's chasing us! It's chasing us!"

Graham looked around and saw the bright light flying toward them from far behind, rapidly gaining on them. "Watch it!" he said urgently, "We don't need to let it get in the tail rotor!"

"Hey man, *you're* flying this thing, not me!" Being new at the helicopter game, Downs hadn't thought about the object getting caught up in the rotor and the possible consequences. Putting some distance between the unknown flyer and the chopper became Graham's first priority. He applied more power, and soon they were streaking over the city at speeds approaching 130 MPH. The object continued to close in.

"I still thought that some moron was recklessly flying a remote-controlled plane," Graham recalls. "So I swung the chopper around in a tight U-turn so that we were flying toward the object. And that's exactly where I wanted it—right in front so I could see it and know it wouldn't hit us from behind."

As the gap between them narrowed, Downs grabbed for the radio, saying, "Kenny, I'm going to call some cars and tell them to come over here, because *nobody's* going to believe us!"

Downs opened the R-4 channel, a car-to-car band that would reach any nearby patrol units, and quickly asked for assistance, saying they were being chased by something and didn't know what it was. Several ground units responded quickly, stopping in a GE parking lot. They radioed back that both the chopper and the UFO were in sight. At this point, the object suddenly veered outward from its path and shot away from them at an unbelievable speed, unexpectedly reappearing behind them once more.

Not again! thought Graham, swinging the helicopter around to face the object, which veered away and disappeared in a flash, just as before. With the excited chatter of the ground patrol units in his ears, Graham glanced behind him, only to see the UFO in its now-familiar position, following them. This time the object did a few maneuvers, circling wide over the GE plant and gaining altitude, then looped back down to their level. Now it was in front of them again, but almost out of sight as they moved toward it.

Downs watched it getting farther and farther away, and screamed at Graham, "It's getting away from us!"

"No, it's not!" Graham shouted back. "It's coming right at us!"

The optical illusions the strange glow created made it difficult for the officers to get a clear sense of which direction it was going. Now it hurtled back toward the chopper—not directly at it, but off to one side. Suddenly, the partners were stunned to see a small fireball shoot from the front of the object, followed immediately by another, and then a third. Approximately the size of softballs, the projectiles were not aimed at the chopper, but instead arched a long, graceful curve toward the ground, dissipating as they fell.

"I thought, 'This *can't* be real!' " says Downs. "But on the radio I could hear officer Mike Smith and other officers on the ground shouting about the laserlike balls."

The UFO continued toward the chopper and decreased its speed as it approached Downs's side, then it bolted out of his field of vision. Graham quickly turned the chopper around again, but all the officers saw was clear, black sky in front of them and in all directions. The mysterious object had disappeared, apparently for good.

Graham and Downs hovered for a few endless minutes, wondering silently what had just happened. That thing was *fast*, Graham thought, as it had managed to fly from one end of the huge GE property to the other in no time flat. Downs quietly radioed to the ground units that they were going back into the heliport.

After landing, the pair said nothing about the incident to anyone, even though it must have been apparent that something had happened. Both were breathing heavily and looked as though they'd just run five miles. In fact, the magnitude of their encounter had just hit Graham, whose mind had been primarily occupied with keeping them and the chopper safe. It was 1:00 A.M., and they decided to call their lieutenant at home to tell him what occurred. They woke him up. After hearing their incredible story, the lieutenant told them to file an incident report and instructed them to have the helicopter checked before they went out again. Graham and Downs knew that an incident report would get the media's attention, and the lieutenant agreed. But he advised them to tell it like it was. "If you say that it was really nothing, then the press will think we're trying to hide something," he noted. "Just tell them what happened. You saw what you saw."

The partners felt better that their boss believed them and was willing to stand up for them. As the helicopter was being serviced, they tried to reason out what had happened, tried to explain it away. But the only alternative they could think of was some sort of balloon, which didn't make any sense. Downs contacted the local airport tower and asked if they'd seen anything on radar. That deepened the mystery—the tower had noticed the helicopter going around in circles all by itself, but nothing else.

The two recalled the strange fireballs that shot from the UFO and appeared to fall to the ground. Could they find them and have tangible proof of what occurred? They jumped into a car and headed for the GE plant.

Both were dismayed to discover the fresh blanket of snow undisturbed, even at the spot they felt certain the fireballs had landed. The ground patrols also helped scour the area and found nothing. As to where the UFO went when it vanished, a paramedic who had been riding with one of the patrol units told Graham and Downs that right after the fireballs were shot, she saw the object rocket straight up into the sky until it was out of sight. So much for evidence. And it turned out the burglary they were originally responding to was a false alarm.

The officers thought the public would surely think they were kooks, and they vowed to remain as silent as they could about the incident, fearing the worst. At this point, Downs was more concerned about their credibility than he was about seeing the UFO. There was nothing left to do but go back and face the music whenever it started playing.

That happened on Monday, and what a concert it was. The public information officer was overwhelmed with interview requests and, following the lieutenant's advice, Graham and Downs obliged. They thought their story would end up as a short paragraph buried inside the paper; they never expected the front-page headline treatment they received instead, nor the national and international attention that followed.

"If a couple of 'good ol' boys' had seen what we did, the press probably would have ignored them. But here were two police officers claiming an incredible experience. The media ate it up," Downs says.

"I didn't want to do press interviews in the first place, but the department felt we had to say something. They stood behind us the whole way."

The story, however, also got blown out of proportion. The wire services managed to cross their wires, and the incident became an aerial "dogfight" between the chopper and a UFO, an account which follows the officers to this day. To make matters worse, a local resident who was a known publicity seeker came forward to tell the press that Graham and Downs had actually seen his homemade UFO, which he'd made from a dry-cleaning bag and some candles. Guess who the press believed?

"The news people started saying we didn't really see anything. They made a big joke out of it, and we got ticked off," Downs recalls. "There's a lot of people who think that a dry-cleaning bag balloon is what we saw. No way. That was no dry-cleaning bag."

At least their fellow officers stood by the pair as well. Friendly joking and kidding aside, the other cops felt that, considering the sources, the story could only be the truth. Says Graham: "We were made fun of on local radio and TV. But the other officers said that coming from the two of us, they know we saw something and had had a strange experience. And to me, that's all that's important. I know what I saw— and even though I don't know *what* it was, I know I saw something extraordinary."

Graham and Downs went about their business. Three months later, Graham's original partner returned to work, and Downs returned to ground duty, passing up an offer to stay in the air patrol because he was quite anxious to get back to the streets. It was easier for them to go about business as usual than most people knew, because in the end their experience did get some more confirmation. Though there had not been any UFO sightings in Kentucky for many years, Graham and Downs learned that another sighting of the same object that had played cat and mouse with them had occurred only 20 minutes later in an adjoining county. Also, a retired police pilot contacted them to say he, too, had once seen the same type of object but had never reported it.

These days, when Kenny Graham is flying at night and he and his observer see a shooting star, it doesn't bother him when his partner says with a grin: "Kenny, we *didn't* see that."

An Incident in Mora County

Livestock ranching is a way of life in Mora County, New Mexico—a rural, mountainous county located in the northern part of the state about 65 miles east of Los Alamos. The area is breathtaking in its beauty, flanked by the Sangre de

Cristo mountain range and the Santa Fe National Forest to the west, and wide expanses of the Kiowa National Grasslands to the east. On its sprawling ranches with miles between neighbors, cattle graze peacefully in the meadows and woodlands. But Mora County, like some other counties in New Mexico, has experienced strange occurrences that have disrupted its simple existence for over 20 years. Someone—or something—has been killing cattle in a bizarre manner that experts, law enforcement, and government officials have been unable to explain.

Mora County Sheriff's Deputy Greg Laumbach also held a part-time job with the New Mexico State Livestock Board. So when he got a call on September 13, 1994, from a hunter who found some dead cattle, he didn't think much of it. He had certainly seen his share of dead cattle killed by predators or even poachers. But Laumbach soon learned that this call involved no ordinary livestock death. When he arrived at the remote village of Chacon, about 13 miles north of Mora, Laumbach was taken aback both by what the hunter said he experienced and by what he himself found at the site.

Larry Gardea had been bear hunting in Lujan Canyon just outside of Chacon on this rainy day. He was on his way home at about 5:00 P.M., walking through a wooded area, when he came upon two cattle. Both appeared dead, and one had been grotesquely mutilated. As Gardea stood in an aspen grove pondering the situation, he suddenly heard a strange humming sound similar to the noise often emitted from an electrical transformer. At the same time, he heard other cattle running and falling nearby. As he looked toward where the sound came from, he was shocked to see a third cow being dragged along the ground by something invisible, which he believed to be somehow connected to the humming sound. He even called it a "sound beam."

"Mr. Gardea seemed to be terrified, but I looked at him kind of funny," Deputy Greg Laumbach admits. "I mean, anybody would wonder how a cow can be pulled through the air like that. But he was insistent that the cow appeared to be

dragged by this sound he heard and that the cow was bawl-
ing and making a lot of noise. When I asked him to go back
to the site with me, he refused to go at first."

Gardea told Laumbach that the "sound beam" pulled the
cow into the wooded area. Panicked, he fired his 30.06 rifle
twice through the brush toward the sound, then fled back to
his home. After some coaxing from Laumbach, Gardea reluctantly agreed to return to the site. Deputy Laumbach was concerned because Gardea seemed to be in genuine fear and, he
says, did not appear to be any sort of kook. At this point, he
felt certain that Gardea had indeed seen something that was
quite terrifying to him.

Dusk was just beginning to gather as they drove through
the forest to where Gardea had seen the mutilated cows. Everything was quiet except for the calming patter of a steady, gentle rain. Arriving at the site, Laumbach could see some fairly
open areas where cattle grazed on scruffy grass. The dense
woods nearby were filled with oak and pine trees, which provided a blanket of leaves and pine needles on the ground.
Everything was soaked from the rain. When Laumbach
stopped his truck, he could see the distinct tire tracks his vehicle left in the soggy ground behind them. Gardea looked appre-
hensive as he pointed to where the dead cows had been. Only
one cow remained, the mutilated one. Walking toward the animal, Laumbach again noticed that their footsteps left impressions in the ground. He stopped a short distance from the cow
carcass and studied the ground around it, then began to walk
in a wide circle around the body.

Laumbach didn't see any signs of human tracks—or any
tracks at all, for that matter. Not even cattle. There was no
sign that anything had driven in or walked around the area.
The ground was pretty wet, and he was convinced he would
have seen tracks if a truck had been on the marshy ground.
Laumbach says: "In the whole area, there was only one set of
tracks—those from my truck. But no tracks of any kind led
right up to the cow's body." And there couldn't have been

tracks anyway, he noted, because there was no way to drive a vehicle through the large trees and thickets behind where the cow's body was located.

Laumbach was more puzzled when he searched for tracks that would show the animal was dragged, as Gardea had stated. There were none, which led to a wild speculation that perhaps the cow might have been lifted off the ground, then dropped in place. "It was like somebody picked it up and set it there, really," says Laumbach. Moving closer to the animal, he began to inspect the wounds, which were the most unusual he'd ever seen.

The cow's body was completely cool, and rigor mortis had set in, indicating it had died at least two hours before. Laumbach examined the head. Strips of skin had been removed from the right side of the jaw, up the side of the face, beneath the eye, around the cheek, and back down the side of the jaw. Half of a nostril was removed. The cuts were very clean, as though some razor-sharp cutting tool had been used. Even stranger was the fact that the cow's tongue had been removed, cut off square right at the point where it connected to the bottom jaw. But strangest of all was the complete removal of the animal's sex organs—both the anus and the vagina had been cut out, cleanly cored as though someone had used an instrument similar to a common kitchen tool for coring apples. Other than a small amount of blood pooled in the bottom of the wound, which was the size of a two-pound coffee can, there was no visible bleeding.

Surprisingly, for all the cutting that had been done, neither was there any blood on the ground. All the cuts were made with the precision of a skilled surgeon. Laumbach had never seen injuries like this before.

"A razor blade could have made those incisions because they were not the toughest parts of the bovine. This was pretty tender skin that had been cut. But they were very clean cuts with no bleeding, and to me that was very unusual," Laumbach says. "In fact, there was a copycat mutilation a couple

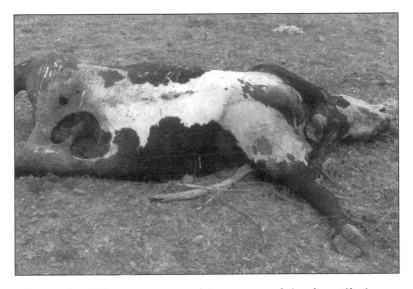

This cow's udder was removed in an unexplained mutilation in northern New Mexico. (NICK SOKOLOFF, COURTESY OF THE SANTA FE NEW MEXICAN)

days later, and the difference between the two was incredibly obvious. The cuts in the second mutilation were real jagged with lots of bleeding and looked like a very random slashing. There was a big difference between the two incidents."

Gardea said that he hadn't seen anything flying around—no helicopters, planes, or anything out of the ordinary. But later that day a couple visiting the area told Laumbach that they had heard a noise that sounded somewhat like jets flying, right at the time that Gardea had heard the humming sounds. "Jets do fly over that area, but I thought it was an odd kind of coincidence that they were hearing these sounds at the same time Gardea was hearing these other sounds," Laumbach says.

At a loss for an explanation, Laumbach went back to the station and wrote up his report, listing the cause of the mutilations as unknown. The sheriff indicated he would send someone else up to take a look, but that apparently never happened. Laumbach says that basically, the whole thing was dropped at that point. It was felt that everything that could be done had been done. Laumbach never could uncover anything more and still considers the incident a mystery.

It was certainly easy for other residents in the little community of Mora to think that Larry Gardea was nuts. They gave him a difficult time, pointing at him, talking behind his back, and saying that the government was going to come and kill him. Gardea seemed genuinely unnerved by the whole affair. In fact, between people's taunts and his wild experience, he decided to "get out of Dodge" and left the area completely. A local journalist who interviewed Gardea about the incident, however, found him to be a very sincere individual.

"He seemed very jumpy. But I thought he was genuine. He didn't appear to be any raving wacko, and I didn't see any reason for him to be making this up," says Andrew Stiny, a correspondent for the *Albuquerque Journal*. "I keep an open mind about the whole thing anyway, because we've had unexplained cattle mutilations like this in New Mexico for a long time."

To try to make some sense of it all, Stiny and other journalists looked back to reports of incidents in the 1970s, the period thought to be the start of such cattle mutilation activity in the United States, particularly in the southwestern states. Incidents similar to Gardea's had been reported even then. In Costilla County, Colorado, two startled deputies had told their sheriff that they witnessed a cow floating through the air in a beam of light. Ernest Sandoval, sheriff of Costilla County at that time, notes that theories of secret government operations abounded back then. He still believes those theories today. His county is located close to the various military bases in and around Colorado Springs. Mysterious unmarked helicopters were commonly seen in connection with the mutilations.

"A rancher and his wife, who had already lost 17 head of cattle to mutilations, once saw a helicopter hovering over one of their pastures and said a man was standing 'on top' of a cow. They were so upset, they drove to my office to get me. The only thing we found when we got back to the site was a puddle of urine where the cow had been," says Sandoval, now retired.

His office and other law enforcement agencies had such a tough time with the myriad of dead cattle that the FBI and the Colorado Bureau of Investigation were called in to assist the investigations. At one point, both agencies called a meeting with sheriffs and police officers from several counties. The audience listened in disbelief as they were told that the mutilations were being done by predators. "We outright laughed at them," says Sandoval, laughing again. He pauses and continues seriously: "The incisions made on these animals were so accurate, so precise, that they had to be done by experts with lasers. I once saw lights above distant pastures at 3:00 in the morning and drove straight toward them. When I got to the exact spot, I found a cleanly mutilated cow. No, it wasn't predators."

People in New Mexico generally dismiss the predator theory as well, says Stiny. He recalls that at one point the State Livestock Board actually declared that the mutilations were *not* from predators. There is also a constant undercurrent of government conspiracy theories and connections to unidentified flying objects. "We hear so many conflicting things. It's a very weird string of occurrences," he says. "In this case, when Gardea went back to the site with Deputy Laumbach and the other two cows were gone, Gardea told me: 'Whatever it was, it came back for the two cows.'"

Though Laumbach has not heard of any other mutilations in the Mora area, there were plenty in the town of Eagles Nest, about 35 miles to the north. Stiny later reported on more mutilations in Taos County about a month after Gardea's experience. Today, Greg Laumbach is a full-time deputy with the New Mexico State Livestock Board. Working in the same locale where he worked as a sheriff's deputy, he has not heard of any other cattle mutilations since. But he still wonders about the one bizarre mutilation he did see.

"It's hard to fake fear, and Larry Gardea was obviously

extremely frightened when I talked to him. His voice was stuttering—he was scared, and there's no way you can hide a fear like that," says Laumbach.

"I don't know if it was a fear of seeing what happened or a fear of what he thought might have done it. It would seem unlikely that someone who regularly hunts bears would just freak out if he suddenly found a dead, mutilated cow. It's not like he's not used to seeing large dead animals.

"But whatever it is he saw and experienced, it was something that really frightened him. I'm still questioning what really did happen out there. To me, the whole thing is still unexplained."

Cattle mutilations around New Mexico as a whole have died off since then. Locals say that the phenomenon comes and goes, with people rarely believing that a period of respite means the end of it. Deputy Laumbach seems to have been lucky that his one experience was, so far, his only experience. But who's to say how long that will be the case?

4

CULT AND
OCCULT
PHENOMENA

IN RHODE ISLAND several years ago, a teenage girl who had run away from home was found in a traumatized state and taken to the local police station. She lay curled in a fetal position and refused to speak. Clutched in her hands was a drawing she had made that depicted a ritual human sacrifice in front of a large sketch of Satan. If the girl had not had firsthand knowledge of satanism, police said, she would not have been able to create such an accurate picture. Slowly the girl began to talk about a recent suicide attempt and her intention to try again, but said little else. Her parents placed her in therapy, where she was said to have spilled the horrifying details of her experience with a satanic cult.

Alarming accounts such as this—and worse—are seen in newspapers across the country on a regular basis. Television talk shows are replete with people telling frightening stories of satanic worship and encounters with occult religions that use magic and sacrifice animals or even humans. Grassroots groups warn of an epidemic, a clandestine movement of everyday people whose lives appear normal on the surface. But at night these same people gather in remote areas to don dark robes, dance around bonfires, drink human blood, and call up the darkest of evils for the purpose of satanic worship. According to these grassroots groups, it's all part of the moral destruction of our nation, and no one is safe from its cancerous spread.

Talk with the FBI, and you get a decidedly different story. Investigators who specialize in cult crimes say there is no evidence to support persistent rumors of organized ritual killings, that not one single body has ever been found as proof of an evil underground conspiracy of devil worshipers. Those who believe there is such a movement claim there are nearly 60,000 victims in the United States who have been sacrificed in the name of Satan. The reason no bodies have been found, they claim, is simply that satanists are so good at hiding the evidence. Law enforcement officials counter those claims by explaining that no bodies are found because there just aren't any to be found, period. Rather than a massive clandestine movement aimed at subverting our familiar way of life, experts say that what's going on is actually a form of cultural hysteria regarding the phenomenon of cults and the occult. The public's imagination running wild is far more menacing in the end.

Which is true? And where do people get these cult stories if they aren't true?

My experience in trying to seek out the answers has left me wondering. While I found it quite easy to locate professionals who were more than willing to discuss statistics and how overblown this matter is, I could not find those on the other side of the issue who could speak openly about evidence to the contrary. I contacted several anticult groups, explained what I was doing, and then waited endlessly for someone to return my phone calls. One did, but that person talked in hushed tones and cryptic sentences about vague notions that, quite frankly, told me nothing solid.

"Where have the bodies been found?" I asked.

"They're all over—everywhere," said the hushed voice.

"*Exactly* where?" I pressed.

"You name it," he replied.

I tried another approach. "There seem to be plenty of

unwilling participants who describe these cult horrors. How about showing me a formerly *willing* participant who changed his mind and brought along hard evidence when he went over the wall?"

The reply: "They don't change their minds."

I was not interested in playing "Twenty Questions," so I stopped after about a half dozen, convinced I was getting nowhere. At this juncture I'm compelled to ask: If there really is a huge, terrible, organized movement of evil going on, why won't anyone lay down the facts they supposedly know, such as names, dates, places? And if the word needs to be spread, why are the people who claim to know the truth keeping all the hard evidence to themselves as though such evidence was a precious secret? I'm open to being informed, but I want more than generalities and nonspecific answers.

Satanism and Other Cults

Experts say the belief that satanism is widespread and well organized is a big misunderstanding, and that there is no evidence to support the claims. The key word is *organized*. There will always be individual dabblers in satanism and occult practices, those who put their own spin on occult concepts for their own purposes. And they often go on to commit heinous crimes in the name of religion, says Dr. Rafael Martinez, a cultural anthropologist and expert on cults and occult religions. But they work alone, he says, and the idea of a larger, unstoppable conspiracy is simply erroneous information being passed on from one misinformed person to another. That information taps into the darkest recesses of the public's fears, provoking gross overreactions.

"Cases of true organized widespread satanic activity are nonexistent," states Martinez, a resident consultant to the Dade County Medical Examiner's Office in Miami. "But there are isolated cases of unbalanced individuals who get hold of literature on satanism, interpret it in their own way, and commit crimes in the name of this religion. Sadly, such cases are frequent."

An example is the instance of three San Luis Obispo, California, teenagers who kidnapped a little girl and admitted to killing her because they needed to offer a "virgin sacrifice to Satan." Besides participating in drug use and dabbling in occult practices, the teens believed that power comes from the sacrifice of a virgin. It could be said that what they did was satanism since it was done in the name of Satan. But Martinez emphasizes that these were individuals acting on their own and not in line with a particular group philosophy. Here is where the misunderstandings on the part of the general public come into play.

"There's no big satanic crusade that's going to overtake the entire nation, and yet some are presenting it as such," Martinez says. "They claim there is an organized network of individuals at all levels of society—including government officials—that systematically and methodically are trying to convert people to their movement. These individuals supposedly offer sacrifices, wear robes, and eat babies. That doesn't exist. Some people actually *want* to believe it exists, but that's another cultural issue. It's like folklore, arising in rural areas like stories of the bogeyman."

Although that information may or may not soothe a few frazzled nerves, it certainly doesn't lessen the overall impact of some individuals' heinous crimes. And those who believe that our way of life is threatened can be pretty convincing, even with their obscure rhetoric. They point to the many people who disappear annually and say that a large number are kidnap victims of satanic cults. Psychiatrists and psychotherapists offer as evidence the repressed childhood memories of traumatized patients. But without solid, tangible evidence to back up these claims, the issue remains one of confusion.

"A good part of this satanic movement phenomenon is based on repressed memory syndrome, and that's just too controversial," says Martinez. "Information coming from such individuals has been gathered by questionable techniques, so there is little faith in their accuracy."

Cults in general, however, do appear to be more out of control these days. One power-hungry individual preys on the weaknesses of others for his own purposes and couches his intentions in the guise of religion. But again, these groups are isolated and small, kept that way so the cult leader can retain control of his flock. Martinez cites the Branch Davidian cult in Waco.

"Would that be called Christianity because they were quoting the Bible?" he asks. "They were a group of people who were deviant and psychologically unstable. They decided to create their own religion that had nothing to do with the spirit of Christianity as we know it. They were dabblers who were mixing religions and adding their own bizarre twists."

While the debate over the existence of organized satanic movements continues, so does the rise of individual deviant cults and their crimes. As law enforcement learns more about the dynamics of such groups, it must still deal with the public's very real fears. Those who believe they are in danger search for answers and perpetrators. This search can lead to trouble if they begin to create their own version of reality. This is where law enforcement can run into big problems.

"If police have absolutely nothing to go on, yet people are convinced there's some evil running rampant, the question in their minds becomes: 'Why aren't the authorities doing anything about this?'" says Martinez. "Aroused suspicions become fears that can grow to unmanageable levels, and that itself is the definition of *hysteria*."

Occult Religions

Some of those fears are often misdirected at occult religions. According to the dictionary, *occult* means "hidden." When applied to religion, says Martinez, occult can be a fairly generic term meaning a religion that uses secret rituals reserved for initiated practitioners to observe. Such religions are not, he emphasizes, synonymous with satanism.

"The various Afro-Caribbean religions found in the United

Offerings to Oshun, goddess of the rivers, money, and love
(COURTESY OF RAFAEL MARTINEZ)

States, such as Santeria, Palo Mayombe, Yoruba, and Haitian Voodoo, are by definition occult religions," Martinez explains. "They are simply different religions from those considered to be mainstream."

These occult religions began in secrecy nearly 400 years ago, when African slaves in the Caribbean were forbidden to practice their own religions. The slaves hid their rites behind the symbols of Christianity until the two religions blended together, or became synchronistic. In Santeria, which is dominant in Cuba, the Christian saints came to represent the true African gods, or *Orishas*. So an offering of coins or cigars to St. Lazarus for health and well-being, for example, is actually a plea for the same to the African god Babalu-Aye.

Unfortunately, these occult religions are consistently and wrongly linked to satanism, says Martinez, and the public really needs to know the difference. The misperception occurs because the unusual beliefs and rituals are not understood, and also because many of these religions include a belief in magic and spells. Much to the dismay of occult religion practitioners, the Judeo-Christian public has difficulty viewing their rituals as those of just another religion.

Cops and the Occult

Even more confusion arises when police who are unfamiliar with these religions incorrectly assume that the activity itself is criminal. A large part of Martinez's work is to educate law enforcement staff in cultural differences and customs to help them distinguish between religious practice, which is a guaranteed freedom, and illegal activity.

"You don't investigate a religion unless a crime is being committed, such as stealing human body parts, which is a misdemeanor," says Martinez. "But practicing the religion and doing the rituals, as strange and bizarre as they might seem, is allowed because there is freedom of religion. Cops can lose perspective and not see where the religion ends and the crime begins."

Palo Mayombe rituals, for instance, often require the use of human bones or remains, so where in the world do practitioners get them? Some believers dig up a grave, which is a crime, or buy the parts illegally. There is actually a market for purchasing those grisly items, which are usually smuggled into the United States from assorted Caribbean islands.

"In Miami, you can buy a human skull for $500," says Martinez. "The act of buying that skull is a crime, but the Palo Mayombe religion itself is not." It's a fine distinction that many people find difficult to discern. It's important to note as well that Palo Mayombe rituals do not always require human remains, and practitioners do not have to follow that very old tradition.

Many criminal drug enterprises call upon beliefs in Santeria and Palo Mayombe for protection of their organizations and activities. Police officers working in that area of enforcement should understand the dynamics of the religions in order to conduct their undercover investigations better, says Martinez. A smuggler might ask his Santeria priest to perform a cleansing ritual on a new warehouse he's acquired to store his drugs. A cop or federal Drug Enforcement Agency (DEA) agent observing these rituals would do well to understand what is going on. This knowledge could also help them recognize any deviant practitioners.

One such deviant was Adolfo de Jesus Constanzo, an individual who practiced Palo Mayombe in his own way to obtain protection for his drug gang in Matamoros, Mexico. Constanzo's interpretation of the religion involved grisly human sacrifices. After the discovery of a mass grave containing 14 corpses, including that of a missing American student, the FBI called in Martinez and his colleague, Dr. Charles Wetli, Dade County's associate medical examiner at the time. Dr. Wetli became well known later as the Suffolk County, New York, medical examiner involved in the investigation of the 1996 crash of TWA flight 800.

"Constanzo practiced Palo Mayombe and not satanism, but he took it a step further," says Martinez. "He was very much into creating his own cult religion incorporating his violent lifestyle and drugs. He was apparently influenced by ancient Aztec religions, which sacrificed humans, because he did sacrifice a number of people. Forensic reports showed that at least four of the bodies were ritual offerings."

The American student had been murdered for his brain. In the Palo Mayombe religion, offerings to the much-feared warrior deity Chango include human skulls. But Constanzo wanted a skull with the brain still inside so that the spirit of the dead, or *kiyumba*, could think better and outsmart the police. Such perverted ideas are often taken as further evidence of cult horrors and their growth, yet, again, they are not part of an organized movement.

While trying to educate both law enforcement and the public about these distinct differences, Martinez knows he must overcome some long-held misconceptions. But the bottom line, he says, is this: "All religions are to be respected, no matter how weird they may appear to us."

Do You Believe in Magic?

What seems oddest to most Judeo-Christians about practitioners of occult religions is their belief in magic, which practitioners claim has great power. I have talked with police officers
who are in close contact with occult religions in their work,
and many say they have personally witnessed occurrences they
can't explain. The officers claim they don't believe in magic
themselves, even if they've seen it with their own eyes. Rather,
they chalk up the cause of unexplainable events to the strong
beliefs of the practitioners.

Magic is the practical aspect of Santeria and other occult
religions, says Martinez. It is an attempt to control what can't
be controlled by other means, to change things that otherwise
can't be changed. The two laws of practical magic are the law
of contact and the law of similarity.

In contact magic, items that were part of the target person
or that have been touched by that person are used in casting
spells. Clothing, hair, and fingernails are examples of what can
be used in rituals to cause health or harm.

"I've seen a Santeros, or Santeria priest, do a healing ritual for a woman who suffered from breast cancer," says Martinez. "He asked her to give him one of her bras for the ritual,
since it had touched the afflicted area of her body."

Items selected should be related to the ritual being performed. If a drug dealer wanted to use ritual magic to silence
an informant about to testify in a trial, he would use some of
the person's saliva. To cause madness, hair would be a good
choice. Martinez recalls an interesting story he heard from a
Miami physician.

"A man suffering from impotence blamed his wife for the
problem. He said she must have taken a pair of his underwear
and used them in a ritual to afflict him," he says.

The law of similarity assumes that like produces like. Rep-
resentations of the target person are used rather than items that

have touched the person. If the target of a ritual is a woman, a female doll would be used to represent her. If the practitioner wishes the woman harm, he might put pins in the doll or cut off the head, says Martinez. The belief is that whatever is done to the image will be afflicted on the target person, or at least something similar.

But the target of rituals don't always have to be people. If someone is looking to buy their dream house, they might go into a botanica—a Caribbean specialty store—and buy a little toy house to use in a good-luck ritual.

"They may have found a house they're interested in, but they want the owner to lower the price. So they could take a bit of dirt from the front yard, put it in the toy house and invoke a deity in a ritual," Martinez explains. "They might call upon Chango, the warrior deity, to fight the 'war' for them."

Does magic work? People who practice it swear it does. There are those who have been arrested and swear that magic helped set them free. Somehow, for some strange reason, the evidence against them got lost or misplaced. No evidence, no prosecution.

In south Florida, the case of a rather successful pair of jewel thieves proved frustrating to police and a bit amusing to the public, but elicited wonderment from both when some light was shed on the duo's remarkable ability to elude authorities. The thieves said they used a Santeria ceremony to become invisible. Despite an expensive three-month undercover operation that included the use of high-tech surveillance equipment, police simply couldn't catch them in the act. The crooks were arrested on minor charges of possession of stolen property, but could not be held on burglary charges due to lack of evidence. Were they really invisible? Or were they just so confident in their beliefs that they were able to perform their criminal activities with astounding ease?

Things that make you go "Hmmmmmm . . . "

I found the following case stories fascinating because of

their cultural aspects as well as their unexplained occurrences. In *"Obatala,"* a police officer who grew up and now works in a part of the country where various Afro-Caribbean religions are practiced has his knowledge and patience put to the test in a bizarre case. Conversely, "Diary of a Mad Housewife" is the story of a detective who knew nothing of the voodoo religions involved in a murder/suicide she investigated, but the victim's diary provided a horrifying look into one man's violent nature and dark journey into the occult. And finally, "Idaho Gothic" is a disturbing glimpse of how cultural hysteria can overtake a small, conservative community and place even local law enforcement officials under suspicion.

Obatala

We knew savage eyes had been watching us,
As onward we had trod.
We showed no fear, though they were near,
We placed our faith in God.
—J. Ed McTeer

Harry Thompson* died in a freak accident on March 2, 1979, a victim of "wrong place/wrong time" syndrome. He was walking down the middle of the street in his hometown of Beaufort, South Carolina, when a pickup truck came up from behind. It passed by a bit too close, and its big side-view mirror hit Thompson with a resounding *thwack*. But that's not what killed him. The mirror caught him in such a way that it twirled him around, and then he could see, coming right at him, a huge piece of farm equipment, jutting out from the back of the truck even farther than the side-view mirror.

Now *that* killed him.

The coroner did an autopsy that showed Thompson had been drinking. His family contested the finding, but the investigation was closed and the truck driver was declared blameless. Thompson's family collected about $22,000 from an insurance policy. Harry Thompson was buried in the city's

Rhett Cemetery, where he rested in peace until late November of that year. That's when Deputy Sergeant Rick Chapman of the Beaufort County Sheriff's Office got a call from Thompson's family saying that someone had tampered with their kin's grave.

Chapman arrived at the cemetery late in the afternoon. It was a small graveyard on the corner of a nice street in a nice part of town. Such family-plot cemeteries are common in Beaufort and throughout the Deep South, where black families customarily set aside some land for family burial. Thompson's family had heard about the trouble with Harry from a church deacon who was gathering firewood at the cemetery and happened to notice that the grave was dug up, the casket exposed. But nobody mentioned what else was wrong at the gravesite, so Chapman was a bit surprised when he found little hex dolls lying all over the grave and hanging from nearby bushes and trees.

Deputy Sergeant Rick Chapman, Beaufort County Sheriff's Office (COURTESY OF DEPUTY SERGEANT RICK CHAPMAN)

"In fact, there were dolls on all the graves, crude humanlike figures made from corn husks and cobs," he says. "They had tiny faces and arms, a note tied around each one with a ribbon, and each was in a paper bag with an article of clothing."

Chapman, who had been born and raised in Beaufort County, knew what it all meant, and as a law enforcement officer, he knew that it was helpful to his work to understand the local religion. He recognized these artifacts as root magic, a type of voodoo, a curse put on the family. None of the other graves had been disturbed, but Harry's had a big piece of plywood lying over the casket, with some dirt piled on top of that. When Chapman peeked under one corner of the board, he saw that the casket had been forced open, apparently by chopping the top off with a hatchet. The police could do nothing more without a court order, Chapman told the family. They would have to see a judge the next day, and then the grave could be examined.

Beaufort County is made up of 64 islands. When the early slave ships broke up in storms off the coast, many of their passengers managed to swim to the islands' shores to safety and made the islands their home. Some of Beaufort's islands are well known, such as Hilton Head for its resorts and Parris Island for its Marine training base. Chapman stated that Danfuskie Island was featured in *National Geographic* because its residents still live in a tribal village tradition. They use a barter system and speak their own language, a mixture of English and African dialects called Gullah. The Africans brought their culture with them, an ancient culture of root medicine that has become part of the very fabric of Beaufort County. Here in the low country, as the area is called, root medicine and magic are taken quite seriously by many people. You can see the colorful signs of its existence in some of the local housing. Doors and window frames are painted purple, yellow, or bright blue—called H'ant Blue—as a safety precaution to protect the resident believers from evil forces.

But mostly the low country is a beautiful, wondrous place with a simple, Southern way of life far from the madding crowds. Lush with live oak trees draped in silvery Spanish moss, it's the kind of place that once you visit, "You'll love it so much you'll want to stay on," Deputy Chapman says proudly. The city of Beaufort was among the cream of the Old South, where plantation owners built their summer mansions with money from cotton and indigo. Today the local economy includes truck farming, shrimping, and crabbing. But some of the old ways are still around too.

The next morning when Chapman arrived at work, he found two headless and bloodless chickens lying by the front door of the sheriff's office, a fairly common occurrence. An older gentleman Chapman knew was standing on the sidewalk, watching with more than a passing interest. Scooping up the chickens, Chapman walked to the trash bin by the curb and said impatiently to the man, "Why you always wasting perfectly good chickens like this?" The man shook his head rapidly in denial—they always denied it. Some relative must have been picked up by the deputies for some type of infraction in the past day or so.

Although Chapman doesn't believe in root magic, a lot of people in Beaufort County do, and he respects that. He has seen root magic curses work on people who believe in it and became scared by it. "It's mind over matter is what it is," says Chapman. "It's a psychological thing. When they put the root on you, they make sure you know about it. They won't come up and tell you, but they'll leave the signs. It puts a fear in you." While the curse itself may not hurt you, he notes, you sure can hurt yourself trying to avoid it. And there's nothing you can do about it until you have it reversed or taken off by

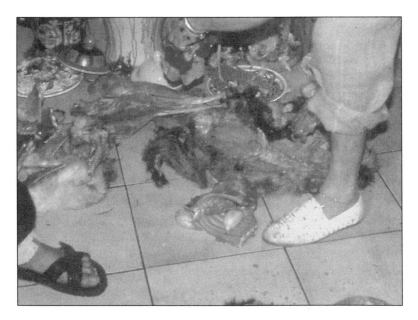

Animal offerings for the *Orishas*, initiation ceremony
(COURTESY OF RAFAEL MARTINEZ)

a doctor. A witch doctor, that is—what many of the locals call a "real doctor," a very powerful figure in their religious beliefs.

The court order finally came through to examine the grave. Chapman, accompanied by Harry Thompson's ex-wife and his family members, returned to the cemetery. Mrs. Thompson kept her back to the plot as the casket was raised to the surface. When Chapman saw the smashed lid, he said, "Ohhh, this doesn't look right." He moved in closer as the coffin was placed beside the grave and the remainder of the lid was pulled back. Now he could see inside.

"What happened? What have they done?!" asked the ex-Mrs. Thompson.

"They removed his head," Chapman replied slowly.

The widow screamed. "Why? Why would they take his head?"

"I don't know."

But Chapman did know. All his life, he had known that if someone was going to put a bad root on you, the way to do it was to dig the grave up and remove a part of the body, like the arm, a leg, the eyes or tongue, or the head. Whoever did this meant business and was out for some *real* bad root on the Thompson family.

Lying in the coffin was the headless corpse of Harry, where the head should have been, a knife was stuck in the satin pillow, a pearl-handled dagger with a very thin, long, razor-sharp blade. Likely it was used to cut off the head, and it did so very cleanly. This was probably a local job and not someone who had come in from out of town just to borrow a head. Right now, the only crime was a misdemeanor grave desecration, though it was certainly a heinous moral crime. But something about this act looked too heinous for Beaufort, and Chapman felt it best to contact the county's retired sheriff of 38 years, Ed McTeer, to find out what he was really dealing with.

Ed McTeer had been only 22 years old when he was appointed sheriff of Beaufort County on February 11, 1926, succeeding his father to become the youngest sheriff in the country. He was a remarkable man, known as the High Sheriff of the Low Country, and everyone believed he was a very powerful man, not only with his words, but in his dealings with the spirits. Ed McTeer was a witch doctor who boasted in his autobiography that he was the only white man ever accepted by black African witch doctors as one of them. Once he retired as sheriff, he worked his magic out of a back room in his downtown real estate office and had a constant stream of clientele. As a Christian, he let it be known that he could only take the root off and not put it on. He never charged for his exorcisms, telling his clients to give the money to charity instead. As another sideline, he wrote several books, including *Fifty Years as a Low Country Witch Doctor* and *High Sheriff of the Low Country*.

There was a time back a few decades when root magic was intertwined with the legal system in Beaufort, and those in the system had to understand how to get around it. The county's attorneys practiced voodoo, mostly because they had to. Prosecuting a believer, says Chapman, usually brought a witch doctor such as Dr. Buzzard to the courtroom. Wearing his trademark purple eyeglasses, Buzzard always sat near the jury and chewed on a root, trying to influence them. Or the attorneys might find voodoo items in their offices—strange powders or tobacco bags filled with hair, crushed bone, coins, or other odd things. They had to fight fire with fire.

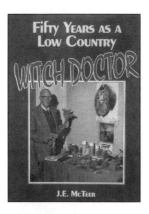

A photo of the late Sheriff Ed McTeer on the cover of his book shows him beside his voodoo altar. An African mask hangs on the wall, and he holds a large root.
(WITH PERMISSION OF JEMCO PUBLISHING, LLC)

When McTeer was sheriff, it might be said that he had an unfair advantage. He used what he knew to get to the truth about root magic. If someone believed in magic, he'd use that belief to his benefit. If a suspect was brought in wearing a voodoo charm, McTeer would take it away, make him real scared. Chapman says McTeer had been trained in the ways of root medicine by a Dr. Hawk, as well as several other doctors who had allowed McTeer into their secret world. But McTeer and Dr. Buzzard were at odds, always trying to outsmart each other. The sheriff hauled the good doctor into court a few times for some of his more bizarre magic practices. For instance, Buzzard would feed red clay to young men who wanted to get out of their military service, or have them drink water with rusty nails in it so they'd get sick enough not to be inducted. Oddly, though, the witnesses against Buzzard usually wound up testifying *for* him.

This was how it was in the low country some time ago.

Ed McTeer looked at the photos of Thompson's grave and listened as Chapman described the dolls and the missing head. The first thing he said was whoever did this was really out to cause the Thompson family some pain, that removing Harry's head signified they wanted death brought to everyone. This was real hatred, he said, and no one questioned what Ed McTeer said. Chapman asked what was the best way to handle all this with the family. McTeer replied that if they wanted to come see him, they could.

Chapman then gathered the family together for a chat. He explained that someone was trying to put a bad magic spell on them. "Now if you believe in it," he said, "then it's going to happen. But if you don't believe it, then you've got nothing to worry about." Some of the family believed and some didn't. It's assumed that those who did went to see Ed McTeer, though Chapman never knew.

That's what made investigating a case like this so difficult. Nobody wanted to say anything about it. "A lot of people run scared. They don't want to know, they don't want to say, and if they do know, they are going to keep it to themselves because they're afraid somebody may come back and try to sprinkle that stuff on them," Chapman says. "People mostly keep their mouths shut. If they do open them, they'll just say, 'Man, you're dealing with something that's beyond you and me, that's more powerful than you and me, and I'm not saying anything about it.' All we could do was watch and wait, ask around and wait for the rumors to kick in."

Slowly but surely, bit by bit over the next two weeks, the information started coming in. Most of the informants began with "I heard . . . " What folks were hearing was something about an argument among Thompson family members over an insurance policy and a small piece of land Thompson had owned. Instead of bequeathing those items to his ex-wife, he'd left them to his brother. Mrs. Thompson felt slighted and angry. She also felt she was entitled to the property. The word was that she had contacted a very powerful doctor, supposedly from New York, and asked how to do the right root for the right revenge. The story, however, was all hearsay, and there was no proof.

The head hadn't yet turned up in Beaufort, though some residents were looking for it. Freshly dug holes could be seen in more than one front yard in town. Locals had heard about what had happened and wanted to make sure the head, along with its death curse, wasn't buried in their yard. Chapman had heard more than once that the head was in New York City, and he decided to follow up on the lead. He called New York City police and explained his problem as best he could. At first, they didn't know what he was talking about, but finally he spoke with a detective who could relate to the situation.

"Hell, we have heads missing almost every day up here," the detective said cheerfully. But unfortunately he didn't have any leads on Harry Thompson's head. He did promise he'd keep an eye out for it, though. "You never know, it might still be around here on somebody's shelf."

With the former Mrs. Thompson denying she knew anything about the beheading, Chapman had no other suspects.

He had no proof Harry's head was in New York, or anywhere else, for that matter. It was a cold case, one that he knew would likely never be solved. All the department could do was sit back, wait, and hope that somebody would come forth to say, "I know what happened." Deputy Chapman wasn't going to hold his breath.

At least nothing gruesome ever did befall the Thompson family, and Chapman never really thought it would, because he doesn't believe in root magic.

He does confess, however, that he once came close to believing. He and other officers were searching for a man who had gone swimming and drowned in a marshy lake. Police divers couldn't locate the body. An elderly man watching the attempts suggested to Chapman that he throw the victim's shirt, which was lying on the bank, into the water, and the shirt would go find the body. "It'll swirl around and spin real fast, then go down and find him," the man said, rapidly tracing circles in the air with his hand. A couple of the deputies chuckled, and Chapman glared at them. He always hated it when the other guys made fun of these people's beliefs.

"Throw it in," Chapman told them. The officers shrugged and tossed the shirt into the water. It floated on the surface for a bit. Then suddenly it started to turn in the currents. As the wide-eyed deputies watched, it spun faster and faster until finally it shot beneath the water's surface. Everyone stared.

"Well, *follow* it!" Chapman shouted to a diver. The man dived down—and surfaced a minute or two later to tell everyone that the shirt had landed almost directly on top of the victim's body, hidden beneath some thick water plants.

Each morning, Deputy Chapman still wonders why people waste perfectly good chickens.

Diary of a Mad Housewife

He frightens me. He excites me. But he also is not the same person I knew before. When I'm away from him, I miss him.

When I talk to him, I feel different. It's like I'm afraid. I'm worried he'll hurt me.

Detective Sharon Lansdowne was riveted to the book. With more plot twists and turns than a good mystery novel, the pages were filled with suspense, obsessive love, jealousy, the occult, and madness. But this was no novel. The spiral-bound notebook was the personal diary of 52-year-old Caroline Mariano Rubia, the subject of the missing persons case Lansdowne had just been assigned in June 1988.

Unfolding before her was the story of Rubia, a mother and grandmother who had worked as an administrator for AT&T in San Jose, California. A prolific diarist, Rubia recorded the daily happenings in her life, including the bizarre details of her *other* life. Behind the job, carpools, and kids' baseball games, Rubia had a dark secret that would shatter the lives of her family and ultimately bring about her strange, untimely demise.

On June 2, Caroline Rubia left on her own from her grandson's baseball game, which had been attended by her whole family. She failed to show up at home. Her panicked husband and an older son went to the San Jose Police Department the next morning to report her missing. They told Detective Sharon Lansdowne that they feared for Caroline's life, having recently learned that Rubia had been having a long-term affair with a man who had threatened her.

"Caroline had tried to break off the affair, but her lover wouldn't get the message. He was becoming more and more insistent that he was still going to be involved in her life," says Lansdowne, now retired from the San Jose Police Department. "We were really alarmed, too, and felt sure her life was in danger."

Lansdowne learned that Rubia's lover had been violent with her in the past and had a history of violence with women. But it hadn't started out that way. Rubia met building contractor Charles William Turner in a bar in 1968, and immediately fell for the tall, handsome, well-built charmer who was five years her junior. Turner couldn't resist petite and attractive Rubia even though he had been living with his girlfriend, Stephanie, since he got out of the Army in 1963. He and Rubia carried on a torrid love affair for nearly 20 years that few people knew about, least of all Rubia's family. But in the last 10 years, their stormy relationship had turned into a fatal obsession, as Turner toyed with the occult and descended into madness.

Lansdowne put out an all-points bulletin for Rubia, her metallic blue 1978 Honda Accord, and Turner, whom she learned had legally changed his name in 1979 to Che François Toussaint. Then she and other SJPD officers headed for Toussaint's home in the nearby town of Campbell. When they arrived, they found the house eerily still. A barking dog was locked in the garage, and there was no sign of Toussaint's truck.

"We got the most ominous feeling about this house. It was locked tight; everything was completely closed up," says Lansdowne. She had a strong hunch that someone was inside, and knew that Toussaint had told friends he'd commit suicide if Rubia ever left him. After summoning Campbell police for assistance, Lansdowne and her squad broke the doorknob on the back door and entered the house.

It was deathly quiet. Though the exterior of the house was lovely and well kept, inside was an incredible mess of junk, old unpaid bills, and, oddly, a massive amount of pennies strewn all over the place. Lansdowne wandered into the dining room area and found more of the same before noticing a strange scene in the living room.

"We discovered an altar set up with candles, more pennies, and a path of notes leading up the stairs," she says. "The notes were to a relative and told what to do with the dog. The front door had been barricaded with a couch and a chair. Now I was certain that somebody was inside. We headed upstairs."

Several rooms branched off the hallway. Two bedrooms were filled with piles of clothing. Searching the den, Lansdowne came upon a small clue to the case. From papers found there, she learned that Toussaint had been treated for valley fever, a disease contracted from airborne spores found mostly in farming areas. The progressive illness can affect the brain and, Lansdowne noted, may have been responsible for some of Toussaint's irrational behavior. Back in the hallway, Lansdowne slid open a closet door and made another bizarre discovery: a second altar filled with strange items.

On one shelf lay three photos of Caroline Rubia, each snapshot covered with a tiny mound of salt. Next to that were three upside-down, quart-sized mason jars, each labeled with a strip of tape. One read "Me"; the next label said "Carol Rubia" and "Stop It!" beneath her name; the third said: "Carol and I." The jars, also covered with salt, held spices and slips of paper with writing on them. One jar contained a brown substance that Lansdowne first thought was blood, but later discovered was molasses.

"At this point, things were getting a lot scarier. We knew nothing about this or what it meant. I thought it might be some kind of voodoo, but I really didn't know," she recalls.

More strange articles were found in the garbage can: a recipe calling for a dirt container, paper sack, tartar powder, red crushed pepper, and three crosses; a "to-do" list reminding Toussaint to "put a dime under couch when have sex," "put salt in my socks to combat evil," "get Tabasco sauce, back up to water and toss it over shoulder," and "a black candle for her to leave." There were pages, torn from the phone book, listing people involved with the occult and psychic phenomena and business cards of occult practitioners. It was clear that Toussaint was deep into something beyond most people's comprehension. Thankfully, Lansdowne thought, Rubia's family knew nothing about this.

What made me become promiscuous? Was it Chuck's good looks and sex appeal that attracted me to him? The psychiatrist said Chuck was probably dominated by his mother while growing up in a home with no father, that he's a macho man who hates and loves women. He said men like this never change. Everything he said about Chuck is so true. He was a mama's boy. She strung him to her apron strings. He threatens me with his women. I can't stand hearing it.

In the last bedroom, Lansdowne found Toussaint lying in his bed. His husky body was a brilliant, flaming red in color, the telltale sign of cyanide poisoning. The voodoo man had carried out his threat, and he did not go gently. Toussaint had likely spent hours in excruciating pain, says Lansdowne. A towel was pressed against his mouth, as if he'd been biting into it. Another altar was in the room, covered with pennies, candles, and voodoo items. A gun found beside the bed had not been fired. "Toussaint was a huge man, at least six feet six inches, but he looked so tiny lying in that bed," Lansdowne recalls quietly. "I'll never forget that crimson color. I'd never seen anyone who looked like that."

Certain now that Toussaint had killed Rubia, the officers thoroughly searched the house but found no weapons or any clues as to where he might have stashed the body. Perhaps the voodoo spells would tell what happened, Lansdowne thought. The whole voodoo atmosphere was bizarre, and she needed to find out how Toussaint had been thinking. She needed to know more about what the spells meant.

He says I'm a witch. He went to New Orleans and spent $3,500 to have someone bring him into the swamps to find out what kind of black magic I perform. He showed me strange things and demanded that I tell him what they mean. I couldn't. How could I? I'm afraid of that stuff.

Lansdowne sought the help of occult experts in San Francisco. They explained to her that voodoo is an African-based religion brought by slaves to the Caribbean and North America more than 400 years ago. Its beliefs and rites blended with local religions—including Christianity in some cases—to create many different sects. Toussaint's voluminous writings on his thoughts and feelings about voodoo revealed a man whose personal beliefs were rather eclectic. He tended to pick and choose certain things he liked from many different religions and occult sects, which made it difficult for Lansdowne's occult experts to learn anything solid from his rituals. One thing she did discover, however, was that Toussaint had been violent in the past toward Rubia and other women and that he was extremely paranoid about Rubia.

Two days later, Toussaint's truck was found in the mobile home park where he had lived with Stephanie. In the front seat, police found bloody prescription eyeglasses belonging to Rubia and a blood-stained newspaper dated June 2, the day Rubia had disappeared. Two days after that, Rubia's car was found at a fast-food restaurant not far from her grandson's school—employees said it had been there for a long time. It seemed quite certain that Toussaint's paranoia had led him to kill Rubia.

"When Toussaint's girlfriend had become ill with multiple sclerosis, he'd abandoned her. She eventually went blind and Toussaint believed that Rubia had caused it all with witchcraft. He told that to all his friends," Lansdowne says. "The things in the jars were supposed to seal in magic and evil spirits, to prevent them from getting to him. He wanted a barrier between him and Rubia in both worlds. Even Stephanie said that he was so afraid of bad spirits that he would cover up her doll collection to smother their 'power.'"

Occult experts felt that Toussaint probably buried Rubia's body in a voodoo manner meant to keep her spirit from arising to get him. Lansdowne pictured a scene where the deep grave would be sprinkled with salt, black candles, crosses, and pins. Salt and pins help keep the spirit confined, said the experts, and the body would likely be tied up as well. But where to find that grave?

I never was so frightened for my life. He threw me to the living room floor, hit me on the sides of my head, my jaw, my ear. I got dizzy and had blurred vision. . . . He was crazy that night. He kept telling me to change and kept asking me to tell him about the witchcraft. I told him I was totally afraid of it and never practiced the stuff. . . . Then he took out a saw and his gun. I was crying, wringing Kleenex in my hands, begging him not to do anything, telling him how much I cared for him.

Lansdowne found that although Toussaint was a bright, well-educated man, he had a vicious side to him. Also, his struggle with valley fever had apparently affected his brain. He thought he was going to die. He was plagued with financial problems related to his construction business and found it reasonable to blame it all on Rubia and witchcraft. Toussaint had once before come very close to murdering her, according to his own writings. "He had taken her into the Santa Cruz mountains with the intention of killing her. He brought a shovel and was going to make her dig her own grave, but then something changed his mind and he decided not to kill her," Lansdowne says. After that terrifying incident, Rubia told her husband about the affair and vowed to save their marriage, agreeing to go off on a Catholic retreat with him to help fix things up. That angered Toussaint even more. When he tried desperately to make contact with Rubia, she rebuffed him.

Perhaps the mountains where Toussaint had taken Rubia before were the place to start looking for the body, Lansdowne theorized.

Police combed the area with search parties, and the Rubia family hired psychics to assist in the search. Nothing was found. Nothing pointed to where the body might be. For the next two years, Lansdowne worked any possible lead or clue in the ice-cold case, with no results.

Then in late March 1989, a family living in the Santa Cruz mountains was stunned when their four-month-old German shepherd puppy dragged home a dirty tennis shoe containing a decomposing foot. The size 5 1/2 white hightop Reebok sneaker was exactly what Rubia had been wearing when last seen. The search was renewed, and local sheriff's deputies soon found Caroline Rubia's grave in an isolated area. "Nobody would have ever thought of looking in that area," says Lansdowne. "If there were any voodoo artifacts on the grave, they had long ago been washed away by heavy rainstorms. It was just a simple lonely grave." Police concluded Rubia had probably been shot to death.

Everyone—including Lansdowne—now had closure. She attended the funeral with Rubia's family. Noting that she'd never had a case like this one before or after, Lansdowne says: "I came away from this somewhat more knowledgeable and with a different feeling about these religions. I wish that I'd known a lot of these things prior to investigating this case. Looking back on my 29 years with the department, I can now see that situations I'd encountered probably had occult overtones that I didn't recognize then. This is certainly the strangest case I've ever dealt with."

It seems that no matter what magic Toussaint had tried to conjure, his personal demons got him in the end. Caroline Rubia was an unfortunate passenger on his willy-nilly journey through the occult. But Toussaint's hold on her approached black magic—through it all, she clung to a love even she couldn't begin to explain, a love she couldn't abandon despite the horrors he put her through. Two weeks before she disappeared, Caroline Rubia wrote the last entry in her diary:

I talk to him every day. Today was real heavy just because I asked him if he's been celibate. I told him for 20 years, I never was with anyone else. I know he still loves me and I still care about him.

There is a bizarre footnote to this strange story: in 1993, outside a restaurant in the Santa Cruz mountains, a patron spotted a small object lying on the ground and picked it up. It was a wallet, filthy and mildewed. The man opened it and found a short note in Caroline Rubia's handwriting:

To whom it may concern, should any harm come to me, due to the circumstances of events as written in my book, it is inevitable that Mr. Che François Toussaint will be totally or partially responsible.

Everything in the wallet was badly mildewed and decaying. Everything, that is, except the damning note and Caroline Rubia's driver's license. They were in brand-new condition.

Idaho Gothic

Baby X

The charred metal washing machine tub and its contents, lying near the landfill in southeastern Idaho, must have been ignored a long time. It was just junk, and the few people who saw it didn't pay it any attention. Little boys, however, love to nose around junk, and this particular junk sat right in the path of one curious little boy. He and his father had to walk past the Minidoka County Landfill to go home after their pickup truck got stuck in the mud just outside the town of Rupert, the county seat. The boy ran ahead of his dad to check out the tub, and whether that was a lucky or fateful act is a matter for debate. But through the darkness of a November night in 1989, the dad heard his son utter a little boyish "Ewwwww!" as he approached the blackened metal cylinder. Dad shined his flashlight inside it, drew a barely audible gasp, and abruptly shooed his son home to bed. Then he called the Minidoka County sheriff.

It took a pathologist to figure out what was in the metal tub, but the forensic report that Sheriff Ray Jarvis read was very clear: the three-week-old infant girl had been dead for less than five days. She had been dismembered, disemboweled, and set afire. She might have been skinned, and all the abdominal organs except the lungs and a piece of her heart had been cut out. The pathologist believed he knew how this happened and editorialized in his report that these horrors were the result of a satanic cult ritual.

This made no sense to Sheriff Jarvis—Minidoka County had no satanists. There were plenty of good citizens whose families founded the town and its many churches—mostly Mormon but also Baptist, Jehovah's Witness, Seventh-Day Adventist, Pentecostal, and more. Sure, every now and then the townsfolk would traffic in rumors of strange gatherings of people along the Snake River, of freaks who danced around bonfires and wore long dark robes. Citizens believed those weirdos were most likely responsible for the dead, mutilated animals that police checked out every time the odd report came in. But explanations were almost always found for the peculiar incidents, which coincidentally seemed to occur around Halloween each year. Sheriff Jarvis always made sure the townsfolk heard those explanations. He never realized, however, that few people actually listened to him.

It's almost a requirement of a small town to whip up some sentiment now and then, to cautiously peer into the night from behind heavy, closed draperies, particularly a small town where everyone knows everyone and little goes unnoticed. But even if things didn't seem right in the town of Rupert, no one had actually seen anything out of the ordinary. No matter that the rumors were about gory things like human sacrifices—usually involving dead babies—no one in Rupert, at least, had ever found a body. There was simply no confirmation of things that go bump in the night.

Not until Baby X was found on November 17, 1989. Now the townspeople had proof of the devil in their midst.

"You Just Never Know What Your Neighbors Are Doing . . ."

The only thing Sheriff Jarvis knew for sure was that he had a bizarre, unexplained murder in his jurisdiction. Despite what the pathologist said, investigators found nothing at the scene to even remotely suggest that satanists were involved.

"There were no pentagrams, no symbols, no satanic messages. I thought those things would have been present because cults like to identify themselves in that way," says Ray Jarvis. "But there was not one shred of proof of satanism. In fact, we had no evidence of anything at all. However, I felt sure somebody in our town knew what had happened and would talk about it."

In a strange way, he was right.

The sheriff's office soon received phone calls and letters

about the case, but Jarvis viewed the contents of those messages with extreme skepticism. People actually accused their neighbors of practicing satanism, of wearing black robes, and of trying to have babies just so they could sacrifice the infants later. Jarvis sent his deputies to follow up on some of the bizarre leads. The men were stunned at what they discovered.

"People stood there in their doorways and said, 'Yeah, we're satanists—so what?'" says one deputy. "It wasn't the whole town, but I never thought there were *any* satanists in Rupert. It really opened my eyes."

Still more troubling letters arrived. One named over 100 alleged cultists in town, including several judges and the local prosecutor. One writer of an anonymous letter from another town claimed to have been a victim of Rupert-area satanists in the past. *"Know that in many cases women were used as breeders for the seed of Satan. . . ."* the letter warned ominously. *"Babies were born in a compound and no records were ever kept. . . . Babies were not dead before disemboweling."*

Jarvis quickly proved that the list of "devil worshipers'" names was copied directly from the local phone book because all the book's spelling mistakes had been included. And other so-called cult evidence had some sort of explanation: a hangman's noose found in an old barn had been made by kids, and reports of skinned dogs turned out to be skinned coyotes.

"People around here hunt coyotes in the winter for their pelts, so that wasn't unusual," Jarvis says. "And the naked bodies dancing around down on the river? Hell, that happens every night here in the summertime—kids skinny-dipping." What about the self-admitted satanists? "They were just young people talking and trying to play the part. I'd known them for years and never saw any signs of devil worship in any way, shape, or form. But all of a sudden when they were questioned about it in this high-profile case, then they were devil worshipers."

About six months after the discovery of Baby X, Jarvis surmised that she was probably the child of migrant workers who had dumped the body and moved on. Traveling farm workers were plentiful in Minidoka County at any given time, and his deputies had found no local hospital records of a baby born that they couldn't account for. Beyond that, investigators had absolutely nothing else to go on.

But none of the explanations and theories quelled the fears of residents who believed there was more to the situation than met the eye. An undercurrent of worry and mistrust existed, but no one could prove anything. By summer of 1990, everyone nearly forgot about the case. That is, until the prosecutor received a phone call in July—a call that would ignite a slow burn under the town.

A Boy Called Timothy

A child protection worker from southern California called to talk about the nine-year-old boy in his custody whom he called Timothy*. The young boy was traumatized, he said, and had drawn some very upsetting pictures and made some horrifying claims. His artwork depicted fires, babies, and, oddly, something that looked a lot like a washing machine tub. His story about watching a baby being sacrificed sure sounded familiar to the rural Idaho prosecutor. He wasn't surprised when the child welfare worker stated that the boy and his parents were originally from Minidoka County, Idaho.

Word spread about Timothy, and matters were made worse when he and his family moved back to Rupert. The town soon discovered the family's beliefs were quite a bit left of center, which really set tongues to wagging. In September, Rupert police talked with Timothy because he had been telling everyone at school about his appalling experiences. The boy said "they" sacrificed animals and babies and that the devil made them do it. When asked to draw some pictures, Timothy created disturbing portraits of groups of naked people and another gruesome drawing that he explained was a baby being cut open to remove its heart.

Almost everyone believed him.

While a newspaper reporter showed the drawings to a psychiatrist, who immediately pronounced the boy to be a victim of ritual abuse, others such as Sheriff Jarvis noticed that details of the boy's stories changed with each telling.

"I thought maybe the child had been led along by some of the adults who questioned him," Jarvis says. "Not only that, the boy suffered from learning disabilities and was difficult to understand. But we followed up on the stories and tracked down every place the family had lived in the state of Idaho. We found absolutely nothing to back up what the little boy claimed he had seen."

The boy's father completely denied everything. Police had no hard, cold evidence that would stand up in court to charge the parents, even after a thorough search of their home. "We turned that home upside down and shook it to see if anything would fall out, and there was absolutely nothing to tie them with Baby X," Jarvis recalls. "But the newspaper and a few individuals in town had made up their minds that the parents were guilty and that we should have arrested them."

The whispers had started. If the sheriff wasn't doing something about these people, there had to be a reason. Just why *weren't* the police doing anything about it? It had been a year since Baby X was found, and the police should have found an answer by now. Could the authorities, too, be part of this conspiracy?

In late 1990, Timothy's family packed up one day, took the boy, and left town.

Wildfire

That should have been the end of it, but there was still unfinished business. Not only was there no solution to the Baby X case, but now no one would ever know what really happened to Timothy. It was obvious he'd seen something horrific, but his secrets were out of reach. That left a bad taste in some people's mouths, and now they doubted much of what they'd always believed about their own community. Just because Timothy and his family were gone didn't mean the evil had left Rupert as well. Something had to be done.

The slow burn was fanned to a blaze in the summer of 1991 by those who believed that the authorities had hidden agendas that precluded them from punishing those who had exploited Timothy. Sheriff Jarvis heard the whispers about himself and the prosecutor—insinuations about their track records and, in Jarvis' case, some very wild conjecture regarding extremely personal aspects of his life. People wanted to know why the Baby X investigation had been bungled. They needed answers.

Great peril—real or imagined—and the terror it caused now produced self-preserving reactions. Ordinary citizens regarded each other with a wary eye, and cautious whispers led to clandestine meetings. Small groups of the fearful gathered to make plans and to combine their strength for what they were certain was a long battle ahead. One group included the coroner, the forensic pathologist, the town police chief (Jarvis's opponent in the upcoming election), a local minister, and a school administrator. They felt the time to act was now—and they used the power of the press to do just that.

It was done subtly at first, without mob mentality. But subtlety was soon replaced by overt actions designed to further spread the fear, says Jarvis.

"The minister walked around town in his police reserves uniform with a gun on his hip. He got miles of media attention for being a pistol-packing preacher," he says. "The press got all the documentation in the case, accused us of not bringing in enough outside help for the investigation, and published a series of articles 'exposing' this whole mythical conspiracy. And they did it right before the election."

The series of newspaper stories provoked angry responses from citizens, who demanded that Satan be stopped. More rumors were generated, and the furor culminated in an emotional candlelight vigil in the town square. The reported crowd of 500 sang and prayed before a massive grouping of television cameras and newspaper reporters. They patted each other on the back for bringing the astonishing truth into the open, the truth being that Baby X was merely a symptom of a greater sickness that was now epidemic in their little corner of Idaho. Jarvis estimated the crowd to be closer to 100, but they were strong nonetheless.

In response to the public outrage in Rupert, the Idaho Attorney General's Office officially took over the Baby X case in late 1991, although they had been involved in and followed the investigation from the start, Jarvis says. They took all the case files, reinterviewed everyone involved—including Timothy and his family—and took Baby X's remains away from the local pathologist to have another autopsy performed "by a real expert," says Jarvis. "It was the best thing they did." The results of the new autopsy were revealing.

The expert refuted virtually everything in the original pathology report. "There was no dismemberment—it was all media hysteria," Jarvis states. "I saw the body at the scene myself and always felt that the heat of the fire caused the body to fall apart. There was also no proof the body was skinned. The attorney general sent someone down to talk to the people in town at a meeting and explain the results. He said the baby probably died of pneumonia, and tests had proven there was not any satanism involved. But I sat in the audience one row away from the newspaper editor, and he just didn't want to hear any of it. That logical stuff doesn't sell newspapers."

The $64,000 Question

During the new probe by the Attorney General's Office, an investigator popped a curious question to Timothy's mother, almost as an afterthought: What kind of stories do you read to your son? The answer cast a whole new light on young Timothy and, by extension, the Baby X case.

"She said she read only one book to her son, a Jehovah's

Witness children's bible," Jarvis recalls. "This included the story of King Solomon, who threatened to split a child in half as a solution to a disagreement. The story had pictures with it that showed a baby being sacrificed and split apart."

The investigator quickly had Timothy examined by an expert in child psychology and satanic cults, who declared that the boy had never been part of any satanic rituals. It was believed that the boy created various versions of what his mother had read to him and drew his own interpretations of the pictures he'd seen. Adults then made their own interpretations of what Timothy sketched and said, and the end result was unrecognizable from its origins. The investigator agreed with Jarvis's theory that Baby X was most likely the child of an illegal immigrant family, that she had died of pneumonia, and the frightened parents had simply dumped the body and moved on.

These conclusions still didn't satisfy those in Rupert who held fast to their beliefs. They felt the only way to bring about change was with politics. Sheriff Ray Jarvis was defeated by the Rupert chief of police in the 1991 election. His 30-year law enforcement career had come to an end.

Life Goes On

Ray Jarvis had started out as the marshal of a small Idaho town in 1962 and soon decided he'd found what he wanted to do for the rest of his life. He had a flair for law enforcement, enjoyed helping people and solving crimes. But 30 years was a long time—including 16 years as sheriff in Minidoka County. After the furor of Baby X, he all but welcomed his defeat.

"I was burned out. Going out to campaign and deal with the politics in that last election was too much—my reserves had dried up," Jarvis says now. "Maybe it was for the better. Maybe my successor can find something in the Baby X case. Perhaps there was something that I overlooked."

One of Jarvis's primary investigators on the case was deeply affected, he says. The man left law enforcement and moved out of town for a different job. Jarvis commends him as a good officer and says he's at least being paid better now. Another deputy remains with the Minidoka Sheriff's Office.

In the spring of 1992, the remains of Baby X were buried in a small ceremony attended by a handful of people. That same summer, in Boise, there was a fire in the state capitol building. A woman who often worked in the building after hours tossed a lit cigarette into a wastebasket, and the resulting blaze pretty much gutted the Attorney General's Office. It also destroyed the records room—including most of the original documentation on the Baby X case.

After the election in Rupert, the Baby X case mysteriously vanished from the local newspapers. Not another word was ever printed, says Jarvis, and he wonders why those who had such a firm belief that this horrible crime had been committed would suddenly abandon that belief as soon as he was out of office. He says he feels animosity toward none and does not feel betrayed.

"I can hold my head up and walk through town knowing I did everything I could," he says.

Some citizens recently approached Jarvis to run for sheriff again, but he politely declined.

"I've done my time," he quietly told them.

In early 1996, three grisly murders were committed in Rupert within a seven-week period. Six people were arrested and taken into custody in those cases. Another murder in a neighboring county may possibly be related. Talk is that there are too many outsiders coming into the county and bringing along their different values of gangs, drugs, and immorality.

Yes, gangs are the problem now—and it's out of control.

5

Disappearances

All over the world, thousands of living, breathing people vanish without a trace from daily life. Men, women, children, and the elderly from all walks of life disappear and, too often, don't reappear. Investigation usually yields at least some small clue that points to a reason or motive. Perhaps a credit card turns up, an item of clothing, or an abductor brags to the wrong person about what he did. But sometimes nothing is ever found to explain why someone was here one moment and gone the next. Occasionally, the circumstances of such disappearances are so strange that they defy logic, and those are the cases that baffle police most.

The emotional destruction caused by these unexplained mysteries can be enormous for the missing person's family and friends. Without resolution, those involved can feel disassociated with life in general because a big piece of it is now gone. It's like the grief experienced with the death of a loved one, only there's no closure because no one can be absolutely sure of what happened. Police may find themselves bound more tightly to a case than perhaps they should be. They may face years of frustration and emotional dealings with families, which makes it very difficult not to become personally involved.

Detectives first look for clues from the missing person's background and associates, but if nothing turns up, they can do little else except spread the word about the missing person as far and wide as possible. They hope someone will see a flyer with the person's photograph on it, or recall seeing the person, or in the worst case have information about foul play involved. Cases can go on indefinitely with very little movement, yet police usually maintain confidence that eventually a solution will be found. Once all avenues have been checked, it becomes a tedious waiting game, and trails grow colder as the wait continues.

But as time goes on, even the most hopeful cop tends to lose much of his or her optimism. Other agencies are often invited to review the case on the chance that something was missed, but rarely is anything new uncovered, and the case eventually reaches a standstill. All police can do is wait for something to surface.

Where Have All the People Gone?

It's frightening how many of these cases exist. According to the FBI, there were 101,330 persons listed as missing in the agency's National Crime Information Center computer system as of April 15, 1997. That's a lot of people. It's as if the equivalent of the entire city of Albany, New York, just up and vanished one day. Where on earth are they? Are they victims of kidnappers, or have they simply taken off on their own? What's truly disturbing about the first scenario is that it implies there are an equal number of criminal abductors running around, free to strike again. In the latter case there's a mystery about the very notion of stepping completely out of one's life and vanishing into obscurity. Who among us hasn't said, "I wish I could just leave all this behind," at times of great frustration or anxiety? Perhaps this is exactly what some of these people did. It's an extreme solution to life's problems, but a solution nonetheless.

An astonishing thought is that it's probably easier to find and recover missing cars, guns, and other property than it is to locate missing persons. The way most cases are solved is when the perpetrator—if there is one—tells someone what he or she has done. The other way is when a body is found. But if an adult person *wants* to be missing, that's a whole other ball game.

If a person has purposely disappeared and fully intends not to be found, odds are great that he or she never will be. Strictly speaking there is nothing inherently criminal about walking away from your life, no matter what kind of grief it may cause for others. Quite simply, you have the right to drop out if you want to. But do you also have the right to stay lost if someone finds you?

Police disagreed on this question. Some said they would not tell family or friends—even a spouse—where the person was if that person didn't want anyone else to know. Cops said they would contact the family and tell them the person had been found and was OK, but as long as no crime was involved, they felt revealing any more might be a violation of that person's rights. Other police said they would tell, depending on the situation. One officer stated he would tell in the case of a missing spouse. But he once solved the case of a boyfriend who disappeared and left his fiancée at the altar—in that instance, he did not tell the woman where the boyfriend had gone.

How often do people escape their identities? Often enough. Modern technology has made it easier in some ways to assume a new identity and to start life over again, leaving your troubles behind you. In certain parts of the country, for instance, it's quite easy to literally buy a new identity—documentation that includes social security cards, driver's licenses, and even credit cards can be purchased on the streets for a few hundred dollars.

When investigating missing persons cases, police are often bombarded with tips from the public about where the people have gone. These tips all have to be checked, and the vast majority will lead to dead ends. Such cases also attract psychics, bounty hunters, and others who may want to capitalize on the situation for some sort of self-advancement. In the case of Larisa Dumansky, who vanished from Sioux Falls, South Dakota, in August 1994, some of the tips have been downright crazy.

"One lead had her running off to Ethiopia," says Lieutenant Gary Folkerts, the investigator on the case for the Sioux Falls Police Department. "Another caller said she left town with a Russian circus, and yet another said she got involved with a 'serial trucker,' whatever that is. Some people even said they could find her by holding some electronic device over a map. It would pinpoint her whereabouts any place in the world. It can get overwhelming."

Dumansky disappeared from her employer's parking lot as she was leaving to go home from her shift. Police found her van, with a flat tire, still in the lot. What happened to Dumansky is complete speculation. She was supposed to give a ride home to a coworker, who was waiting for her at the main entrance to the meat packing plant where they worked, but she never drove around to pick him up. Her keys were found dangling in the car's door lock. Despite the number of people who were leaving the plant at that time, not one person saw anything unusual.

Lieutenant Folkerts found there was nothing at all unusual about Dumansky, either. She and her family had fled the Soviet Union because of religious persecution and had lived a completely normal life in the United States. He couldn't come up with any reasons why she might have wanted to leave on her own. Because of this, he theorizes that someone she knew abducted her without using force.

"I'm convinced it's probably someone we've already interviewed—and we've interviewed hundreds of people in this case," says Folkerts. "She either knew the person or accepted an offer of help with the flat tire from someone she didn't know. But we've checked everything and come up empty. I can't think of another case this department has put more time into."

High Emotions

Missing persons cases can eat at the psyche of both police and those close to the one who has vanished. The cases often drag on for years—sometimes decades. No cop likes unfinished business, but too often these cases remain unsolved.

In western Pennsylvania, one police chief has been haunted for 15 years by the disappearance of two small boys whom he knew. The kids, ages 10 and 11, went outside to play after dinner one night in 1982 and were never seen again. By now, the chief says, the boys would be in their late 20s, if indeed they are alive. "Cold" doesn't even begin to describe the case, which has seen much change since the beginning: the FBI agent who became involved has retired; a missing children's organization that assisted in the search has been disbanded; the children's parents have moved on with their lives; and the police chief has grown older and more frustrated. After so much time has passed, what can be done that hasn't already been done? Living with the mystery of "his" boys' disappearance for so long, the chief's personal pain is apparent. Though technically the case is still open, he no longer wants to discuss it. The mere mention of it made him agitated.

Dealing with victims' families can also be downright heartbreaking. Caught in a painful limbo, all they really want to know is what happened to their loved one. Even if the person took off purposely, knowing that fact would be easier to deal with than knowing nothing at all. Part of the pain comes from constant hopes that the person will return. Another part is fear that the person is in need of help, and the family is powerless to do anything.

Lieutenant Curt Schram of the Michigan State Police knows this all too well. He has been investigating the case of two men who vanished while on a hunting trip in late 1985. The most unusual aspect of the case, he says, is that not a trace of Brian Ognjan or David Tyll has been found since then, not even the black 1980 Ford Bronco they were driving. Despite five-figure cash rewards offered by the families for information on the case, no new tips have materialized. Police have long suspected foul play, however, and were able to identify some potential suspects in the disappearances. Informing the family of the situation was very difficult, but the march of time has been worse.

"That's probably been the toughest part about the whole thing," says Lieutenant Schram. "The father of one of the missing men passed away from cancer several years ago. He wanted to know where his son was, but he died not ever knowing what happened. That was a real tearjerker."

Both police and families of missing persons cling to the hope that the person is still alive, and often their hope is what keeps them all going. For police there's a lot of dedication involved as well, because after a point, all they can do is wait.

The two missing persons cases presented here are about as baffling as they come. Hopefully, in the not-too-distant future, the families of Philip Taylor Kramer and David Churchill Jackson—and the officers who are still searching for them—will find the answers they seek.

Missing: Philip Taylor Kramer

Philip Taylor Kramer had an appointment on February 12, 1995. The six-foot, five-inch, 42-year-old electrical engineer and computer entrepreneur had to go to the Los Angeles airport to pick up a business associate flying into town that morning. The meeting had to do with the new life of Kramer's company, Total Multi-Media, Inc. (TMM). A year before, Kramer filed for bankruptcy protection, but now was restructuring the firm and getting it back on its feet again. The high-technology field of computer software and digital video was full of economic ups and downs. Now the company's hopes rode high on Kramer's new research in video recording and playback, research that was being termed a breakthrough by those who knew about it. Kramer was in a positive mood when he left his Thousand Oaks home that morning, bidding a cheery good-bye to his wife and two children.

Philip Taylor Kramer never returned and has not been seen since.

Senior Deputy Tom Bennett of the Ventura County Sheriff's Office was assigned to the case. He admits having little to go on except for a number of strange circumstances that became more bizarre as time went on. These occurrences raised a number of possibilities about what happened to Kramer, but there is absolutely no evidence to back up any of them. Bennett, sifting through the myriad of potential scenarios, was left with some difficult questions: Was Kramer alive or dead? If dead, had he been murdered, or did he take his own life? Had he been kidnapped? Did he assume a new identity and leave his life behind? Or had he gone mad?

"Kramer vanished without a trace. For all we could find out, this was not a man who would ever do anything this irresponsible on his own," says Tom Bennett. "He consistently had been very responsible and thoughtful of the people around him. But his van has never turned up, and his ATM cards, credit cards, and cellular phone have not been used. He's just gone."

Philip Taylor Kramer, missing since February 12, 1995 (COURTESY OF KATHY KRAMER)

Kramer had been a visionary who saw the future of computers and video. In the 1970s he was a musician, the drummer for the popular rock group Iron Butterfly. As the music industry changed, Kramer used his considerable intelligence and entrepreneurial talents to form TMM, a multi-media company, with some friends. TMM struggled, but Kramer's ideas were sound, and the firm emerged from its bout with bankruptcy with a good future still ahead of it. People enjoyed doing business with Kramer. He wasn't necessarily a bad businessman, and market conditions apparently had had a lot to do with the company's problems. Mostly, people liked Philip Taylor Kramer simply because of his upbeat personality.

A stable family man with a loving wife and two children, Kramer was active in his kids' school and coached his son's hockey team. He was close to his parents as well, often work-

ing on high-tech projects with his father, a retired professor
of electrical engineering. With everything going for him, no
one could make sense of the peculiar events surrounding his
sudden disappearance on February 12.

That morning, Kramer left home early so he could stop at
the Los Robles Regional Medical Center to visit his father-in-
law before going on to the airport. He left the hospital at 9:30
A.M. and made several calls on his cellular phone while driving to Los Angeles. Kramer spoke with his wife, Jennifer, and
told her that his friend's plane would be late. He wouldn't be
able to pick him up after all, he said. He told her that when
the man called, Jennifer should tell him to take a cab to the
hotel. Kramer would then see him later at their planned dinner meeting at the Hyatt Westlake Plaza in Westlake Village.

Then the phone call took a bizarre turn.

"He told Jennifer that he loved her, he always had loved
her, and he was never going to see her again," Deputy Bennett says. "He offered no explanation as to why he said that,
and she, of course, became very upset." Kramer then brushed
off his own statement. He went on to say that he had a big
surprise for his wife, and he'd see her at the hotel that night.
Later, he phoned her again and said cryptically, "Whatever
happens, I'll always be with you."

Jennifer wasn't the only recipient of odd calls from Kramer
during that time. He phoned his close friend Ron Bushy, Iron
Butterfly's original drummer, and told him, "I love you more
than life itself." He also spoke with his mother in Ohio. Then
he made a final, chilling call. At 11:30 A.M., from the Ventura
Freeway in the Agoura area, not far from Thousand Oaks,
Kramer dialed 911.

"This is Philip Taylor Kramer, and I'm going to kill
myself," he announced. He was never heard from again.

Suicide? While Kramer did many of the things suicidal people tend to do, such as call relatives and close friends for a last
chat, he hadn't given anyone the slightest indication of any
kinds of problems, except for the veiled comments to his wife.

No one who knows him believes he actually did away with himself. Nor do they believe he could possibly have killed himself and hidden both his own body and the dark green Ford Aerostar van he had been driving. But Bennett isn't so sure.

"Kramer loved the outdoors and enjoyed hiking in very remote areas in the hills around here," he says. "If he had gone to such an area with the intent of killing himself, it would only be a matter of time until someone stumbled on his body. But that could be a very long time as well."

Kramer's family organized an intensive search of the Santa Monica Mountains and beach areas that he loved so much. Bennett himself spent many hours in a helicopter flying over the hills. But no trace of Kramer or his van was ever found.

Could the business have had anything to do with his disappearance? Although the company made it through the bankruptcy proceedings, it was known that Kramer was deeply troubled by his business woes. His family did not believe this was a factor in his disappearance, however, and discounted any theories that revolved around possible bad dealings. Bennett says he has found no leads in Kramer's business affairs.

Despite the happy appearance of Kramer's family life, Bennett had to consider the possibility of Kramer having had an extramarital affair. It isn't unheard of for a man to vanish with another woman. But no matter where he looked, Bennett found no evidence of that.

"Everyone I talked to, from his current friends and business associates to old friends from his Iron Butterfly days, told me that Kramer is the most monogamistic man they've ever met," he says. "When he was with the band touring on the road, and he was dating a girl back home, that was it—she was his girlfriend. And only when that relationship was over would he talk to anybody else."

Bennett focused his attention on the two hours between 9:30 A.M., when Kramer left the hospital, and 11:30 A.M., when he made his last cellular phone call. Those two hours were technically unaccounted for. He was driving around and going out of his way to make phone calls to a lot of people, and he no longer had to go to the airport. But where was he during that time and what had he done? Bennett's investigation led him to information that only further deepened the mystery.

It turned out that Kramer had gone to the Los Angeles airport after all. Although he never picked up his business associate, parking lot records show that he spent 45 minutes at the airport. A parking attendant clearly remembered seeing him leaving alone. How did the attendant know who it was? Kramer signed an IOU for the $3.00 parking charge in order to leave the lot.

"It wasn't unusual for him not to carry much money," says Bennett. "His father said Kramer borrowed some money from him the night before to take his kids out to dinner. We discovered they never went."

The prospect that Kramer had been kidnapped was examined. If he had been so close to a breakthrough in the often cutthroat field of high-technology electronics, a kidnapping didn't seem like such a crazy idea. But no one ever made any ransom demands, and Bennett firmly believes that Kramer's family had been completely honest about that issue. Besides, he says, "If Kramer had been 'abducted' at the airport, his abductors wouldn't have put themselves in a situation where Kramer would have to sign a promissory note for parking."

Friends and family members soon received sporadic phone calls in which the caller simply sat on the line in silence. Thinking it might be Kramer, they pleaded with him to speak and urged him to come home. But Bennett believes the calls were pranksters who were somehow moved to fluster the family after seeing all the local and national media attention the case received. Then Bennett himself got calls—literally hundreds of them—from people who thought they saw Kramer in the Los Angeles area and elsewhere. At one point, reports poured in placing Kramer in 80 different locations in the Western Hemisphere, from Puerto Rico to New York to Colorado. Welfare workers in Sacramento said he visited them to obtain food stamps, while psychics reported their visions. One saw Kramer being worshiped as a god on a California Indian reservation.

"We were flooded with calls," says Bennett. "I never realized how many six-foot, five-inch people there are in this world. I found out it's not as exceptional as I'd originally thought." He did not discount every sighting, however. There were some that he could say with certainty were false leads, but others he couldn't know for sure one way or the other without checking them. All Bennett could do was contact local law enforcement agencies and let them know that Kramer had been seen in their jurisdiction.

The baffling clues in this case led to a great deal of speculation, and neither Bennett nor Kramer's family dismissed any theory, no matter how outlandish. They considered that he might have been whisked into a government protection program of some kind, but Bennett says a person's whole family goes underground in such cases. Kramer's mother speculated he had been hijacked and taken to South America. Why? She simply said that in this day and age, people disappear in South America all the time. Kramer's sister, Kathy, who had devoted herself full time to searching for her brother, thought he may have suffered a form of amnesia brought on by exhaustion and weeks of little or no sleep. From such theories, the family's pain and desperation were apparent.

Today, Tom Bennett seems to lean a bit more toward one particular scenario: for whatever reason, Philip Taylor Kramer decided he just wanted to change his life and get away from everybody and everything that he knew in California. It has looked that way all along, says Bennett, with no signs of foul play. Wherever he is, Bennett feels he is there by his own choice. But if this is the case, Kramer's reasons for leaving in such a startling fashion pose as much a mystery as the enigmatic pieces of his disappearance puzzle.

"If I were able to locate him," Bennett says, "I would urge him to contact his wife and his sister at the very least, to talk with them and let them know what's going on. For the family, having to deal with all of this and just not know what's happened, well, it's got to be miserable. The worst part is what the family is going through. I really feel for them."

Pick a scenario—any scenario. People can deal with any event as long as they know for sure what happened. If Kramer left on his own and his family were to know that he's alive and well, they could handle the situation, as painful as it might be to know that he doesn't want to see them. Not knowing is pure heartbreak. Tom Bennett continues to pursue this as a missing persons case; Kathy Kramer is still actively involved in keeping the search for her brother in the public eye. And Philip Taylor Kramer—wherever he is—is sorely missed by everyone who knows and loves him.

Philip Taylor Kramer, born July 12, 1952, is six feet, five inches tall; weighs approximately 220 pounds; and has brown hair and blue eyes. Kramer has a distinguishing scar under his chin, and his upper front teeth are crowned. Anyone with information regarding this case should contact their local police department, which will, in turn, contact Detective Bennett, if warranted.

Missing: David Churchill Jackson

David Jackson was excited about seeing his five-year-old son, Johnny. It had been some time since they'd last been together, but Jackson's ex-wife had just called from Arizona to say she was bringing the little boy back to Florida to see his dad. The timing of their visit was perfect—Jackson and his roommate, Al Bracho, whom he'd known for over seven years, had just moved into a great new apartment in Pembroke Pines, near Fort Lauderdale. To inaugurate their new home, Jackson had bought some new furniture and had invited friends over to help him assemble the entertainment center. Work, too, had been going very well. As a driver for Coca-Cola for the past four years, Jackson had a good income and job security with a solid company. All in all, life was pretty good. So good, in fact, that blond-haired, 24-year-old David Jackson was all smiles, and he wanted to celebrate.

Right after work on Saturday, June 25, 1988, Jackson called his stepfather to get a favorite recipe for chicken parmesan, so he could cook an extra-special dinner when his son arrived in less than two weeks. Later that evening at about 8:00 P.M., he asked Al Bracho to lend him two dollars because he needed to go get a pack of cigarettes. Bracho obliged, and as Jackson walked through the door, he called out, "See you shortly!"

David Churchill Jackson never came back.

Al Bracho became concerned as the evening wore on and his roommate hadn't returned. By the next day, he knew something was terribly wrong. Jackson was very close to his mother, Judith Carlson, his younger brother Mark, and his sister Angela. The fact that they had not heard a word from him was incredibly strange. When Jackson didn't show up for work Monday morning or even call in, his mother notified the Pembroke Pines Police Department.

"Everyone felt there was no reason in the world for David to run off on his own," says Detective France Michaud. "It didn't appear that he'd planned to go anywhere since he left the apartment with only the clothes on his back and the two dollars his roommate had loaned him. David took his car, and that was all."

Detective Michaud was assigned the case two days after Jackson was reported missing. By this time police already believed that foul play was involved because Jackson still had not contacted his family or anyone at work, nor had he picked up his last paycheck. His girlfriend, who also hadn't heard from him, was so concerned that she stayed temporarily at his apartment, hoping he would show up.

Michaud set about building a file on David Jackson, looking into his past—who his friends were, what his regular activities entailed, and what type of personality he had. She learned that Jackson was a well-liked young man who lived up to his

David Churchill Jackson, missing since June 25, 1988
(COURTESY OF JUDY CARLSON)

responsibilities and had never been in any trouble. All of his friends and relatives described him as reliable and predictable, always keeping in close touch with his family. He had no major financial problems and always paid his bills on time. If he needed extra money, he would work overtime hours to earn it. Jackson shunned drugs, did not have any mental problems, and was never at odds with the law. He was what police would call "perfectly clean."

A 1982 graduate of Hollywood Hills High School, Jackson got married only a year later. That marriage lasted for 18 months, but before it was over, his son Johnny was born. The split was difficult for Jackson, as he loved his son, and it was especially difficult when his ex-wife and son moved out of state. But he kept in contact and treasured the times he and the boy could spend together. After the divorce Jackson moved back home and lived in one of his family's efficiency apartments, located behind their house. He always paid his room and board on time. Whenever he walked past the house on the way to his apartment, he would call out to his mother, "I love you, Mom!"

In May 1988, Jackson and Bracho decided to get an apartment together, and Jackson hugged his mom as he told her about it.

"Are you sure it's OK if I move out? I know I'm your favorite and all," he said with a wink.

"Of course it is," Judith Carlson insisted, and jokingly added, "I'd say it's about time, too. Then I won't have to lie awake at night and listen for that click of the doorknob." She never dreamed she'd soon be lying awake listening for the phone to ring with news of the whereabouts of her child.

Detective Michaud tried to trace where Jackson went to buy cigarettes after leaving his apartment. She located and questioned a truck-stop owner who remembered seeing Jackson on the day he disappeared, possibly the day after. He felt certain it was Jackson he'd seen because he remembered a tattoo on the man's arm. Jackson had a very distinctive one on his upper right arm: a tropical scene of the beach, a palm tree, and the sun. The man said Jackson bought a pack of cigarettes, then got into a black Toyota Celica that had a sunroof. The vehicle description matched Jackson's car, but the lead turned into a dead end. Several other sightings of Jackson also went nowhere. Reports of sightings would continue sporadically for the next several months.

A few days later, Jackson's brother, Mark, called Michaud to tell her about some odd phone calls he and some other people had been receiving. The first one had been to Al Bracho's mother, and the unknown caller had simply sat on the phone without saying a word. The phone rang again a few minutes later, and this time a menacing voice said, "Your son better be careful, or the same thing will happen to him as David Jackson." A third call after that was also nothing but silence.

Mark Jackson got calls on a daily basis from someone who would not talk. He believed it was his missing brother, and as hope overtook him, he pleaded into the silent receiver, "David, you've *got* to talk to me!" The calls continued for a week until someone finally spoke. A deep voice abruptly warned, "Leave your brother's disappearance alone!"

Says Michaud: "We never could find the source of the phone calls. But whoever it was knew enough to contact David's brother."

Then one night, Mark Jackson had a dream.

Mark vividly saw his brother in the woods, crying. Two men had dragged him there, shot him in the head, and dumped his body into a canal. Incredibly, David Jackson's girlfriend also had a similar dream. Mark became convinced that both of them had received a message. But where was the canal located?

South Florida has a large, complex system of canals. Nevertheless, Mark Jackson spent the next several weeks searching every canal he could, swimming with a mask and snorkel through waters that are often home to alligators and poisonous water snakes. He found nothing. But before giving up on Mark's haunting vision, the family contacted a psychic in an attempt to gain further insight. Without any previous knowledge of Mark's dream, the psychic amazingly described the same death scenario, adding that the canal was near a white picket fence. Mark eventually told Detective Michaud about the dream, but no such canal was ever located.

Apparently, someone had been keeping an eye on Mark Jackson's public efforts to find his brother. He got another strange phone call on September 19. This time, a deep voice said, "Your brother is dead. Leave it alone." It was a complete surprise after so much time had gone by, and Mark said, "I was scared to the point where I just shook."

As if circumstances weren't peculiar enough, David's car was discovered two days later at the Fort Lauderdale Airport.

"David's black Toyota Celica was found in the long-term parking lot, properly parked and secured," says Michaud. "It had been there for 35 days, since the end of August, fully two months after David disappeared." The doors were locked, but no keys were found. A pack of cigarettes was in the console tray, a six-pack of beer sat on the floor of the passenger side, and two nylon tote bags with some personal belongings were found in the back seat. The crime lab searched the car thoroughly but found no hair, blood, or fingerprints—not even Jackson's. The case was about as cold as it could get.

Michaud listed Jackson in the National Crime Information Computer. For the next several months she tried to track him through his credit cards and social security number. But none of those items had been used since his disappearance. She checked with old friends of his who had moved away from the area and sent flyers to any place in the country where Jackson knew someone. In the spring of 1989, she started to receive calls from other states reporting sightings. "I was spreading the word as far and wide as I could," she says. "David's friends in other states were shocked to hear that he'd vanished. But no one had seen or heard from him."

In May, a potential suspect in the case turned up. Michaud spoke with an ex-girlfriend of Jackson's, who had seen him prior to his disappearance. The woman was in the midst of a nasty divorce made nastier by her refusal to sign uncontested divorce papers. On May 21, her husband had called to threaten her and said, "I can kill you. I can take you out. I can take a contract out on you and make you disappear like David." Thinking there may have been some bad blood between Jackson and the woman's husband, Michaud quickly had the man brought in for questioning. He denied any involvement.

"In spite of what he said in his threat, we had nothing to pin him to David's disappearance. He admitted to seeing flyers about David and said he'd be willing to take a polygraph, but he later declined to take the test on the advice of his attorney," she says. Not long after, the man committed suicide.

Michaud was at a loss. For the next two years, she followed any leads that came up. Finally in August 1991, she employed the services of another psychic. Though she had never worked with one before, Michaud asked Kay Marko* if she would help her. She did not tell Jackson's family she had done so.

Marko held Jackson's personal address book and told Michaud that Jackson was associated with people who were into bodybuilding. She saw two women in his life, saying that they were more interested in him than he was in them. Marko also believed she saw items that could have suggested narcotics and described two males who were either of Indian descent or mulatto.

"The psychic went on to say that she didn't believe David was alive or that he would ever be found," Michaud says. "I confronted the family with this information just to see if anything at all fit, but nobody had any knowledge of it. In situations like this, one always has to wonder if the person might have had a life that no one else knew about. But at this point, I was certain that something terrible had happened to David."

The most unusual case Michaud has ever worked in her 12 years in law enforcement is still open. Her best theory is that David Churchill Jackson was abducted, possibly by someone he knew. For whatever reason, these people felt compelled to do away with him and then to unconscionably taunt his family. There have been no solid clues since 1992. But Michaud continues to work on the case in hopes of someday helping Jackson's family reach some sort of closure.

"I wouldn't be going through all this if I'd thought David had left on his own," she says. "But if he did and has taken up a different identity, that would mean he's completely abandoned his family that he was so close to. The question then becomes: why?"

Sadly, Jackson's family believes he is dead. But with no solid proof one way or the other, there is always a glimmer of hope. It is possible for someone near and dear to us to have a life we know nothing about. But in the case of David Churchill Jackson, it's more likely that he was in the wrong place at the wrong time with the wrong people. Despite his run of good fortune at the time, he was somehow destined to encounter one moment of bad luck. No matter what occurred, Judith Carlson just wants to know the truth about her son. And she's made her intentions very clear: "I have no plans on dying until I get an answer."

David Churchill Jackson, born September 24, 1963, was 24 years old when he vanished from Pembroke Pines, Florida. He is six feet, three inches tall, weighs approximately 168 pounds, and has sandy-blond hair. He was last seen on June 25, 1988, and was wearing a cut-off T-shirt, bermuda shorts, and sneakers. On his upper right arm is a distinctive tattoo of a palm tree, beach, and sun. Anyone with information regarding this case should write to Detective France Michaud, Pembroke Pines Police Department, 9500 Pines Boulevard, Pembroke Pines, FL 33024, or call (954) 431-2225.

6

OTHER
UNEXPLAINED
PHENOMENA

IN THIS CHAPTER are several stories of other unexplained phenomena, two of which are cases with circumstances *so* unexplained as to defy categorization. "Katherine" is the story of a lingering mystery in Alabama involving the murder of a young woman in 1980. The popular college student was missing for 48 hours before her body was found, but its condition still has police wondering exactly what happened during those two days she was gone. "The Grave of Harry Spitz" relates the strange case of a burial vault and casket that burst through the ground in a West Virginia cemetery 20 years ago. The cause of the eruption is still unknown.

The other two stories were not easy to obtain, but each has some fascinating background on its subject that's worth detailing. Poltergeist activity and sightings of strange creatures were the two most difficult subjects to get cops to talk about on the record. As you read about these phenomena, you'll see why.

Poltergeist Activity

The toll of poltergeist activity on people can be truly astounding. In the instances where this phenomenon appears, the lives of the people experiencing it can be ruined. Besides the extreme terror of dealing with fantastic occurrences that can include moving objects, disembodied voices, horrifying apparitions, and even spontaneous fires, victims of poltergeists wrestle with the possibility that the bizarre events were brought on by something they themselves did. Often they are subjected to an insensitive public and press who invade their privacy. The sheer madness of what can occur physically in poltergeist situations, however, makes people eager to see such paranormal events with their own eyes before they are willing to believe those who are experiencing it.

The first reaction of many who hear of a person's experience with poltergeists is to assume that the victim is making up a story for some reason. Rational humans know that the horrors depicted in the popular movie *Poltergeist* can't really happen, right? I confess to having had a great deal of skepticism myself on this subject until I listened to several police officers relate their experiences. All had a tendency to talk in a hushed tone throughout the conversation. Many would hesitate to make certain statements. Most admitted fear, and I could hear it in their voices—real fear is something you just can't hide. Though I have yet to see poltergeist activity myself, I am no longer a nonbeliever.

Just what is a poltergeist? Parapsychologists are divided on that question. The word *poltergeist* is German and, literally translated, means "noisy ghost." Many parapsychologists, however, believe that ghosts have little or nothing to do with the phenomenon. The commonly accepted theory has its roots in psychology. Poltergeist activity is an expression of psychic forces derived from the subconscious mind of a person around whom the phenomenon is occurring. Generally, that person is an adolescent or prepubescent child and most often a female. In the 1960s, psychologist Dr. William Roll of the Psychical Research Foundation in Durham, North Carolina, conducted studies on poltergeist activity that included psychological testing of subjects who were experiencing it. The results of his work were published in his classic book *Poltergeist* (*not* to be confused with the book on which the movie was based). Roll identified interpersonal crisis as a "red thread" that ran through all the cases studied. Today, most parapsychologists accept this psychologically based theory.

Other researchers believe a poltergeist is a completely external force that is drawn to a particular person who acts as some type of conduit for it. This theory has some merit in cases where poltergeist activity is so violent and extreme that the human mind could hardly be considered responsible. It seems, though, that the gap between the two theories is closing a bit as researchers on both sides question long-held beliefs.

"Many now doubt whether a distinct line can even be drawn between spiritual phenomena such as hauntings or apparitions and poltergeistic activity," says Peter Jordan, a psychologist, researcher, and field investigator with the Psychical Research Foundation. "I have to confess that what gives me pause sometimes are the extreme cases such as fire poltergeists and others in which the magnitude of the phenomenon seems to argue against such a facile explanation as a psychologically based theory."

It's difficult to reconcile flying objects and grotesque apparitions with simple psychological factors. Yet those theories have great appeal because people are trying to hold onto rational and reasonable explanations. In the case of extreme activity, however, "There is something that urges, almost *demands,* that we relinquish that hold and admit to the very strong possibility that we're dealing with some discarnate entity or force which may be deriving its power from the poltergeist focus," says Jordan.

We can add to the mix the possibility that naturally occurring phenomena might explain a lot of what is thought to be poltergeist activity. Controversial theories such as ball lightning, plasma gas, and piezoelectricity do offer potentially reasonable explanations, says Jordan.

"Transient electrical disturbances such as ball lightning have been documented in cases thought to be poltergeistic. A ball of silver, red, or bluish light floats into the house through a window, and seeks out an electrical conduit through telephone wire or a fuse box. The fuse box then literally explodes with flames coming out of it," he says. "The plasma ball is seemingly under some intelligent control or of supernatural origin, but that's not so. Ball lightning can cause tremendous fires, but we have yet to know why it forms in some locations and not others."

The origins and configurations of plasma phenomena are hotly debated, even though conventional physicists accept its existence. Jordan likens its study to that of quantum physics, the principles of which are very elusive.

"Everything in physics is for the most part speculative and inferred," he says. "Subatomic particles have virtually no dimension to them, so they are almost inconceivable by a human. How can something exist that doesn't have dimension to it? The only thing we can do in a field like that is make predictions about how certain phenomena will behave based on what we know. We look for those patterns, and when they exist, that is considered to be confirmation of the theory. In the case of these natural phenomena, I believe they impinge on some of these subatomic areas. That is why the answers are so elusive and why these things don't behave according to conventional rules."

Is it really this complicated? Yes, it is. So imagine what happens when police or arson investigators, who don't have the benefit of a parapsychologist's knowledge of poltergeist activity or of a scientist's understanding of quantum physics, try to place this activity into some sort of reasonable category they can understand. They're completely at a loss as to the cause. Even though it's not their job to figure it all out, they do have to deal with it on a personal level, at least as far as understanding the victim goes. If police do become involved in these cases, it is usually as protectors of the victims and the community from the onslaught of curious outsiders.

Just ask Chief Douglas Glamann of Horicon, Wisconsin. In 1988, a local family experienced a horrifying poltergeist ordeal that brought international attention to his small town of 3,600 residents. The media was hungry for details of the family's tribulations, which they say included inanimate objects moving about the house, visits from glowing apparitions that spoke and threatened family members, and fires of unknown origin. While his department was not involved in investigating these activities, Glamann did talk with the family at length, mostly to determine for himself how true these outlandish occurrences were. He was convinced that the family was indeed going through a very real trauma.

"I absolutely believed them," Glamann states. "But I had to be satisfied that they were being forthright about what was going on. This family wanted nothing more than their privacy, so my role became one of protector while their ordeal played out. I even ended up fielding money offers from the media to the family for their exclusive story, but they wanted no part of any of it."

The locals didn't help either. As time went on and people's imaginations and fears ran wild, Glamann caught wind of rumors that somebody planned to burn the family's house down. On top of dealing with the press and the outsider invasion, he was compelled to post 24-hour guards on the house and work 16-hour days himself. But all the while he couldn't shake his own curiosity about the mysterious occurrences in the house.

For years Glamann insisted neither he nor his officers witnessed the strange phenomena. Now he confesses that he held back from the press. Otherwise, he says, he might have lost control of the situation. Reporters had asked specifically if he ever saw a large, frightening apparition the family described, and he had said no.

"But they *didn't* ask if we'd seen or had an unusual experience in the house. They were too specific," he says. "To get the right information, you have to ask the right questions." Glamann credits years of testifying in court for his tap-dancing abilities.

So what exactly did he see? Glamann had visited the house with one of his officers, the town mayor, and some local clergy who planned to do a blessing ritual.

"Shortly after we entered the house, the phone started to ring incessantly," he says. "We'd answer it but no one would be there; we'd hang up, and it would immediately ring again. This went on for about five minutes before it became annoying. The other officer finally took the phone off the wall, put it on a table, and broke it apart by unplugging the receiver and the main cord to the wall.

"It was completely disconnected, but it still rang right there on the table."

Everyone agreed not to say anything about the incident. Additionally, another officer had a frightening experience in the basement of the house that he later related to Glamann. The officer said there was one area where he felt as if he couldn't breathe.

"He said it was like a tremendous weight on his chest that knocked all the air out of him, but if he moved to a different spot, it went away," Glamann says. "He played around with it a couple times, then walked all through the house to see if there was anywhere else he could feel it. There wasn't—it was only that one spot. This officer was the naysayer in the whole deal and is not at all superstitious."

The harried family moved out of the house after a month. Since then, Glamann has become an unintentional expert of sorts on poltergeist activity. Each year around Halloween, newspapers everywhere rehash the Horicon story from a standpoint of wondering what's going on with the house now. Those yearly articles compel people from all over the world to call Glamann for advice about their own poltergeists.

What's interesting is that he gets so many calls, that there really are so many cases of poltergeist activity going on at any one time. We just don't always hear about them. But police do, as they can be among the first to be called to the scene and sometimes the last to have a clue about what's going on. It's important, therefore, that information about research into this obscure area be brought forward so that those who find themselves in such situations can know where to turn for assistance in investigating.

The poltergeist case in the story "Fire House" was extremely horrifying to those involved. I wish to note that the people who owned the house no longer reside in the area.

Cryptozoology

We don't know exactly what it is, but it has many names—Yeti in the Himalayan Mountains, Skunkape in the American South, Yowie in Australia, and the Wild Man of China. Native North Americans call it Sasquatch, and its legend is nearly as old as the creature is thought to be. Sightings of a great, hairy apelike beast wandering through wilderness areas have been reported in every state except Rhode Island and Hawaii and on every major continent of the world except Antarctica. The sightings continue to baffle and frustrate cryptozoologists, those researchers who seek to prove the existence of strange, unexplained creatures.

The wildest tales warn that Sasquatch is not something you want to meet unexpectedly in the woods—although the creature has begun to receive some positive media coverage in recent years. (The film *Harry and the Hendersons*, starring John Lithgow, portrayed it as quite unabominable, even cuddly.) But none of the sighting accounts—at least the ones that serious researchers consider to be authentic—involve any contact or interaction with the humanoid beast. It is usually spied from afar as it scrambles to hide from view once again, though some sightings have been within several yards of it. There is nothing to indicate the creature wants any contact, as it always moves away when it sees a human. Sasquatch, it seems, doesn't want anything to do with us.

Many researchers believe the North American Sasquatch is a gigantipithicus, a prehistoric creature of Asia that may have wandered to North America over the land bridge that once existed across the Bering Strait. Some think it's a lost creature indigenous to the continent. And, of course, many people believe it's a hoax. But such a lengthy one? The first recorded sighting in North America was in 1811 by a Canadian government worker. Stories of Sasquatch were passed on to Lewis and Clark by their Indian guide, Sacajawea, who told them of large tribes of hairy Indians in the northwest. Further back than that, the Viking explorer Leif Ericksson supposedly wrote in his log of encountering a large tribe of "hairy men" on his first day on the North American continent. Theodore Roosevelt even wrote about a sighting in his book *Wilderness Hunter in Idaho*. Who several centuries ago had time to go around hoaxing other people, and what did they have to gain?

Assuming Sasquatch is a real creature, everything that is known about it points to something primate, something that has managed to survive for millions of years without a lot of evolution. That's just the type of creature cryptozoologists seek out, along with sea and lake monsters such as the alleged creature in Loch Ness. The truth is that new species (or old ones thought to be extinct) are being found all the time. Of the 80 known living species of whales and porpoises, 11 were discovered in this century, with the latest one found in 1991. In 1992, three animal species believed to be extinct for millions of years were discovered still living, says Larry Lund, a noted Sasquatch researcher from Seattle.

"A herd of over 200 oxen thought to be extinct was discovered in Thailand, along with the Moonjack, a saber-toothed type of deer with long tusks," he says. "And in the same area, scientists have rediscovered another deer species called the Slow-Running Deer."

With a name like that, they should have found it a long time ago. Which brings up a point: How can creatures such as these—and creatures like Sasquatch—go on existing undetected for so long?

In the Pacific Northwest between Seattle and San Francisco, 44 aircraft have gone down since World War II, everything from small single-engine prop planes to commercial airliners. None of them has ever been found, says Lund. Nor have we found D. B. Cooper. So it shouldn't be difficult to believe that a real creature such as Sasquatch could exist in the wilds without being caught. "A cunning, nature-savvy human can easily avoid other humans, so why can't Sasquatch hide as effectively?" Lund asks.

This photo of "Big Gal," shot near Portland, Oregon, in January 1967, is considered to be the only authentic photo of a Sasquatch creature—that is, it has never been disproved. The creature was seven feet tall and, for some reason, was believed to be female. (AP/Wide World Photos)

Because no one can get near the creature, some researchers and enthusiasts almost wish a Sasquatch would get hit by a car—such gigantic roadkill would certainly make the case for its existence. A few people actually advocate shooting a Sasquatch to get the final proof.

"Could I shoot one? No way!" says Lund. "What if it was the last one?"

Lund has never seen a Sasquatch though he has seen three different incidents of footprints. He says the research is getting more serious, and attempts have been made to find hairs from the creature to test using DNA technology, in hopes of determining exactly what kind of animal it is. But even hair has been impossible to get, so for now the only means of studying the creature is by recording the accounts of those who have seen it.

There are many police officers who claim to have seen Sasquatch, but most will not elaborate on their experiences. I found this to be the one subject almost no one would discuss. For some reason, Sasquatch sightings seem to carry more potential for serious ridicule than any other subject I've covered. Part of the problem may be how easy it is to perpetrate a Sasquatch hoax. Lots of people do it, so most sightings are immediately labeled as such. Whoever reports seeing one of these creatures is made the butt of jokes. One officer had what he said was a remarkable sighting, but he declined to elaborate, saying his Native American beliefs forbade him from doing so. Three other cops just said they didn't want to bring the subject up again. But a fourth who had clammed up for 20 years about his experience did agree to talk. His story follows in "The Creature of Whitehall."

As you read Officer Brian Gosselin's story, consider this: There are still areas on our world maps that are labeled *unexplored*. We simply don't know every square foot of our own environment or what might be living there. So it's best to keep in mind that although we can't prove with certainty that Sasquatch exists, neither can we prove with equal certainty that it doesn't.

Katherine

It's not common knowledge that the city of Mobile, Alabama, began celebrating Mardi Gras in high style more than 100 years before New Orleans did. Students from the local campus of the University of South Alabama looked forward to the annual celebration as a diversion during the long period between Christmas holiday and spring break. In February 1980, Katherine Foster spent several days enjoying what was to be her last Mardi Gras. For two Mobile homicide detectives, it was the beginning of a baffling case that has left unanswered questions, doubts, and mysteries to this day.

Katherine Foster was studying for a degree in physical therapy. The petite, blonde, blue-eyed woman was popular and had many friends on campus, mostly old chums from her Pasacagoula, Mississippi, high school. Sometime around 11:00 A.M. on Thursday, February 21, Foster met her friend Becky Townsend* in a neighboring dormitory to go on a shopping trip. Suddenly she realized that she had forgotten something back in her own room. "You finish getting ready," she told Townsend, "and I'll meet you in the parking lot shortly."

Major Wilbur Williams, Mobile Police Department
(COURTESY OF MAJOR WILBUR WILLIAMS)

Just before noon, Townsend arrived and waited in the parking lot, but Foster never came. After an hour of searching for her, Townsend called the campus police. They found no sign of Foster and officially reported her as missing to the Mobile Police Department later that evening. Police don't generally start an intensive search for an adult right away, as adults are liable to go off on their own from time to time. But they felt the need to begin looking right away in this case, since Foster's friends and relatives had seen no sign of her, and the girl was not the type to disappear. Major Wilbur Williams of the Mobile Police Department says there were major concerns from the start, and by the next day the department had launched an all-out search.

To effectively search for a missing person, says Williams, police must learn all they can about that person's activities and associates. Extensive information gathered on Foster painted a picture of a perfectly normal person. Raised in a strict Catholic home, she had attended parochial schools and was very close to her church and family. All of her friends had similar backgrounds and habits, and police found no sinister relatives or associates in her life. Foster's long-time boyfriend was well known and liked by her family. She had no unusual habits or pastimes and was not the kind of person to run off somewhere without telling anyone.

"Without question," says Williams, "something was terribly wrong with this situation. We decided to do a very detailed search of the university grounds the next day. This was no small feat."

Wooded site where Katherine Foster's body was found in February 1980 (COURTESY OF MOBILE, ALABAMA, POLICE DEPARTMENT)

Indeed, the sprawling 200-acre campus in west Mobile had many wooded areas and a large number of buildings to search. Campus police and volunteers were enlisted to help out, and the media spread word of the search efforts. By Saturday morning, a crowd had gathered to look for Foster. It didn't take long to get results. Sometime between 11:00 A.M. and noon, Foster's body was found in a wooded area just northeast of her dormitory, lying on her back, dead from two gunshots to the head. The area around her body was fairly undisturbed, but police did find two sets of footprints leading into the small thicket of trees—one set belonging to Foster, the other presumably her assailant's. From the position of her body, it appeared that she had been forced to kneel and had been shot in that position. But beyond that, police were baffled by some very strange and inexplicable circumstances that emerged from the crime scene.

"This is really difficult to explain, but Katherine Foster looked as though she'd been suspended in time," says Major Wilbur Williams, still mystified after 17 years. "Except for the two gunshot wounds, everything about her was undisturbed. Her makeup, her clothing—she was dressed in exactly the same clothes she wore the day she disappeared, and they were as fresh as the moment she walked out her door. It appears as if she just remained in some type of suspended animation from Thursday to Saturday."

She had not been dead for long—there was a bit of rigor mortis, but it was easily broken. Yet if she had been alive for nearly 48 hours since her disappearance, why weren't her clothes wrinkled or disheveled even a *little* bit? The very act of moving around should have taken its toll on her freshly pressed clothing. Could she have been naked all that time? Strangely, the results of later medical examination made that possibility unlikely. Time of death had been placed at approximately eight hours prior to the discovery of her body. Aside from the expected lividity on the body's backside, there were no bruises, cuts, or scrapes, nor were there any indications of a struggle, bondage about the hands or feet, or gagging of any kind. There was not a mark on her.

Toxicologist reports revealed no presence of any known narcotic substance in her body, no alcohol, nothing foreign. There was no sign of sexual activity, either forced or consensual. But the medical examiner did find an infection and, after contacting Foster's personal physician, the case became even stranger.

"This absolutely baffled us—she had some type of vaginal infection. As a result of this, her gynecologist said that inevitably she would have shown some discharge on her underclothing had she worn them for several hours," says Williams. "That discharge should have been there or at least evidence of it—it was not." The medical examiner did find internal presence of the discharge, but as long as Foster had been living, breathing, and moving around, the discharge would have come out. Although no one could prove what underwear Foster had on the day she disappeared, police could prove that the rest of her clothing was the same she had worn that day. It was a good assumption the underwear had also been put on at that time. And the possibility that she had been naked was already shown to be unlikely.

Police are quite certain of the time frame during which the girl died. At around 2:00 A.M. Saturday, nearly two days after Foster vanished, a student who suffered from asthma had opened her bedroom window for some fresh air and immediately heard what she thought were two firecrackers exploding. Fireworks noises are common during Mardi Gras time, so the student thought nothing of it and went back to bed. At about the same time, a campus security officer seated in his car at a nearby intersection heard what he, too, thought were two firecracker explosions. The time, 2:00 A.M., was right in the middle of the time frame set by the forensic examiner for Foster's death.

Although the two stories matched, police found it odd that they could not re-create the shooting to jibe with the witnesses' accounts. A person standing where Foster was found fired a gun similar to the one used in the killing, while two other persons were placed in the witnesses' locations—yet neither one could hear the gunshots. Weather experts explained that atmospheric conditions were unusually thick the night Foster was shot, and that may have caused the gunshot sounds to travel in different ways than they normally would have. This situation only frustrated investigators more.

By now Williams and another detective, John Boone, were certain that Foster had been taken against her will but without a struggle. It's a proven fact that a vast majority of homicides are committed by someone the victim knew in some way. Incidents of people murdered by total strangers are few in comparison. This fact would indicate that Foster either knew and trusted her abductor, or she felt obliged to leave quietly with the person because the killer held some sort of authoritative position. The number of possibilities was endless, but no matter which direction the detectives turned, they found nothing.

Williams and Boone followed ice-cold trails for the next eight years. Since the Mobile Police Department did not have a "cold case" team, the pair tried to work the case into whatever time they could find amidst the new homicides they investigated.

"This just hung over our heads. The unknowns far outweighed the knowns, and we got nowhere," Williams says.

In 1988, the pair was sent to investigate a case that should have blown Foster's murder mystery wide open, but to their distress, it only added *more* questions.

Joseph Quigley*, a security guard at the university campus, had committed suicide. Upon arriving at the man's home, the detectives found bizarre evidence that led them to classify Quigley as the first viable suspect in the Katherine Foster case.

At Quigley's house the detectives discovered a trove of paperwork relating to Foster's death: piles of newspaper clippings, copies of her autopsy report and other public-record information about her case, and original material such as poetry that he had written about the young woman. Quigley obviously had had more than a passing interest in Foster's death. Even more stunning was the fact that he had actually been interviewed during the investigation years before because he had been working on campus the night she was shot. But nothing about that interview made investigators suspicious of him in any way. Now Quigley was dead, and a new question was raised. Foster disappeared at a time when he was proved to have worked two full shifts. If he had indeed taken her, it would seem he'd had an accomplice. Otherwise, he would have had to restrain her, and from her seemingly untouched body, all experts had concluded she'd never been restrained in any way. Quigley had carried a gun issued by the campus police department, but its large caliber didn't match the weapon used in the crime. He had no personal firearms registered to him. Baffled, detectives now moved their search to a garage adjacent to the house. There they made a surprising discovery.

In the attic of that garage was an enclosure, a chicken-wire cage that appeared to have been designed to hold a person. A bare mattress was on the floor inside it. But the cage was woefully inadequate to truly hold an adult, says Williams. He doubts that Foster could have been left there alone. The wire was so thin, it could have been bent easily to effect an escape, and it certainly allowed noise to pass through. Quigley's property was surrounded by other occupied houses. If Foster had been left in that cage ungagged and unrestrained, she would only have had to holler and anyone outside could have heard her clearly. If she'd tried to rip the wire down, she would have at least skinned herself, broken a fingernail, cut herself—something that would have shown up on her body.

Says Williams: "I don't care how docile a person might normally be. Under confinement, the instinct for self-preservation would eventually overtake anybody. But Katherine Foster was unmarked."

It was learned that Quigley's mother had also committed suicide, and so had others in her family. The accomplice theory stubbornly remained—perhaps Quigley's mother not only knew about the crime but had participated in it, guarding Foster at night when her son was working. Aiding Quigley in his bizarre venture may have contributed to her suicide. "Put the mother into the equation—it's safe to assume they were both crazy as hell. It almost figures out. But for everything that pointed in Quigley's direction, there were an equal number of things that negated them," Williams says.

Mobile police asked the FBI for a psychological profile on Quigley. He turned out to be "a damned good suspect," says Williams. He certainly fit Williams's theory of an authoritative figure that Foster would have gone with if asked to. They may even have known each other, although no link between the two was ever found. The reality was that police may have simply stumbled on someone who apparently had some really weird hobbies and who may indeed have been a nut. But whether he was involved with Foster's murder never was and never can be proved. Quigley may simply have had a fetish from afar for dead young women, in which case the newspaper clippings might have been nothing more than a truly bizarre coincidence. In the final analysis, says Williams, "he either did it or he didn't. And if he didn't, who did?"

Williams and Boone spent over 10 years together and investigated more than 360 homicide cases. Each one had its unique characteristics, but the Katherine Foster murder has proved to be the most challenging of all.

"It's frustrating as hell to have a case that you can't bring to a resolution. I always wonder, damn it, was it something I did? Something I didn't do? Was there a piece of evidence there that we just stumbled and bumbled over?" Williams wonders. "But reality sets in, and you have to tell yourself that you do the best you can with what you've got. Yes, there are going to be those cases that end up unsolved. I still pick up newspapers and read about a case here, a case there, and if there's *any* shared resemblance to the Foster case, I go digging at it, trying to find a connection. But the truth is we know little more today than we did back then."

Williams classifies crime victims into two categories: just victims and true victims. Those whose lifestyles put them at constant risk of becoming the victims of crime are just victims. The drug abuser who buys her thrills in the worst part of town; the prostitute who climbs into anyone's vehicle to turn a trick; the gangbanger who runs with the criminal element—all risk becoming crime victims themselves. Katherine Foster was a true victim, one who did not live a life of risk, who did everything right, followed all the rules, and, perhaps, trusted a bit too much. It's been 17 years, and it seems like a lifetime for Williams and Boone. But it also seems like only yesterday that Katherine Foster disappeared alive and reappeared dead, after a two-day stopover in some strange limbo the detectives may never comprehend.

The Grave of Harry Spitz

The Fourth of July 1975 was approaching, and in the green-blanketed Appalachian Mountains of West Virginia, the city of Morgantown prepared for its annual holiday bash. Everyone was looking forward to picnics, parades, and the usual fireworks explosions. Sometimes, people shoot off fireworks in the darnedest places, and some of the bombs and rockets folks tend to pick up in Ohio—the kind that aren't legal in many of Ohio's neighboring states—can be really powerful. That was the first thing Glenn Pierce, the caretaker of Morgantown's Oak Grove Cemetery, thought about as he squinted against the morning sun, trying to see across rows of tombstones to a small pile of dirt in the distance, a pile of dirt that shouldn't have been there among the neatly manicured plots. As he neared the site, he thought maybe someone had been blowing up bottles or setting off some other fireworks. No, maybe someone was digging over there—a thought that really disturbed him. When he finally stood beside the gravesite, Pierce didn't know what to think.

Morgantown Police Department Officer Ralph Chapman and Oak Grove Cemetery superintendent peer into the grave opening, looking for clues to what happened.
(RON RITTENHOUSE, THE DOMINION POST)

In 23 years of caretaking, he had never seen anything quite like this. Sometime during the night, an unknown force had caused a burial vault to burst through the ground above it. Pierce quickly called Morgantown police to report the incident as vandalism. When Chief Bennie Palmer and Officer Ralph Chapman arrived at the scene, however, both were stunned by what they saw. The ground was torn and buckled, pushed upward apparently by something from beneath the earth's surface. It didn't look at all like someone had been digging—all the ground had broken the surface from underneath. They also saw no signs of an explosion, as Pierce had suggested. There was nothing obvious to explain what had caused the heavy concrete vault's lid to pop to the surface.

"It was a real mystery. The grave had actually burst open from within. There just weren't any signs of tampering from the outside," says Ralph Chapman, now retired from the

Morgantown Police Department. "We didn't find any evidence of charred earth or gunpowder residues, either, even after intensive investigation."

Thinking there may have been a natural gas explosion, Chief Palmer contacted the gas utility company to come by and check for leaks. As he waited, he surveyed the scene. The grave was located in an older part of the cemetery, in an area where a road had been built several years before. During construction, the ground surface had been graded down a couple of feet, so the grave was actually shallower than the standard six feet. Palmer could see that a corner of the vault had split apart at the seam, skewing the box's angles and causing the three-inch-thick cement slab lid to break loose. The lid had canted upward and to the side, creating a gaping eight-inch hole through which they could see into the broken vault. Peering inside with a flashlight, Palmer and Chapman saw a tiny casket. Whatever force had caused the vault to move must have been quite strong, yet the casket was still sealed and apparently undisturbed by the vault's movement.

"At first I had thought that maybe gases from a decomposing body had caused the site to erupt. But we could see that the casket was sealed shut, so that didn't seem likely," says Chapman. "That day, I filed a report listing the cause of the eruption as unknown. Over the next couple days, we had a lot of people try to figure out what had happened, including folks from West Virginia University, but no one came up with any answers."

Chief Palmer recalls that from time to time a strange group of people had been seen holding meetings and seances at Oak Grove Cemetery. His officers would come by and run them off, but they kept returning. "To be quite honest, when we first got this call, I thought those weird people had done something during the night, like set off some kind of explosive device," says Palmer, also retired from the force. "But again there was no evidence of such a device. Then the gas company arrived and checked for leaks, but found none. They also probed the streets on two sides of the cemetery and found nothing there, either. It was really baffling."

Palmer contacted cemetery management, several funeral directors, and the prosecutor's office for permission to exhume the grave. The casket needed to be reburied in a new vault, but now they wondered who was lying inside. There was no marker at the grave site, and an initial search of grave maps didn't provide a name. The site was located among several graves belonging to a family named Spitz. Cemetery administrators assumed there might be a connection to the family, but records covering that part of the cemetery had been lost or destroyed years before.

Chapman says a local news reporter followed the Spitz family lead. He soon was able to identify the casket's occupant as a three-year-old boy named Harry Spitz, who had died of cholera 63 years before. Now the short life and family history of the child was unveiled.

"The boy had relatives still living in the area who gave us permission to exhume and rebury the casket," says Chapman. "It was a very interesting story about who the child was, and it made me wonder even more why something like this had happened."

Harry Spitz came from a family of German immigrants who had settled in the area in the early 1900s. His sister Irene was now 59 years old and still lived in Morgantown, as did his 91-year-old mother, who was in poor health and a patient at the nearby state hospital. According to Irene, little blond-haired and brown-eyed Harry had been a happy child who loved to play with toys. He looked a lot like his father, who had worked at the local glass factories. But Harry's life was cut short when he contracted the croup, or cholera infantum, in September of 1912. He died eight days later and was taken to the Oak Grove Cemetery in a horse-drawn hearse. His death devastated the family, and Harry's mother was in deep mourning for years after the child's death. Palmer recalls seeing some old photographs of Harry's funeral, which was well attended, especially by many young children. The police pondered this information and the mystery before them. Here was a little boy who had died a sad, horrible death. Was there any reason in the world for his final resting place to be disturbed in such a violent manner? And what on earth—or below the earth—could have caused it?

Workmen remove casket from the grave of Harry Spitz.
(RON RITTENHOUSE, THE DOMINION POST)

The exhumation brought no answers and only raised more questions. In one last attempt to find a cause for the eruption, workers opened the casket. What confronted them posed an even more baffling mystery. Inside were indeed the remains of little Harry Spitz, but in a remarkably preserved condition.

"The body still had intact skin and was not in the bare-bones state, which it should have been after all that time. In fact, you could recognize Harry from his facial features. He even had lots of long blond hair," Chapman says. "The skin appeared a bit leathery, but the body was extremely well preserved and that was very strange indeed."

Palmer says Harry wore a blue-and-white outfit, and there was a little stuffed lion at his feet, apparently the child's favorite toy. A small engraved plate inside the casket read, "Our Darling," and an identical plate was found on top of the casket. In the little boy's hands were some flowers, dried and brown. While the casket lid's fabric had rotted away, everything else inside was remarkably well preserved. And no one could explain why.

"The vault was handmade and crudely constructed. There was a company that made vaults in the section of town where the little boy had lived, and this one was likely made there," Palmer says. "I could see very faint newspaper columns printed along the side of the vault. The makers likely used newspapers to line the vault form so that when they poured the concrete, it wouldn't stick. But I thought it was really strange how the vault could withstand the elements for all those years, then just suddenly break apart with such force. It just didn't make sense. And the wooden casket inside was in good condition."

The morgue supervisor from West Virginia University Hospital took tissue samples from the little boy's hand to determine if there were any living organisms on the body. None were found, confirming that body gas could not have been the cause of the grave's eruption. Those results were corroborated by Dr. Nathaniel Rodman, then chairman of pathology at

West Virginia University. Dr. Rodman added that body gas *could* have been a consideration within one or two years of burial, but not after 63 years. He confessed to having no idea what had caused the grave to open up.

Another theory put forth proposed that a methane gas explosion might have ripped the ground open, but there were no hints of the presence of that gas anywhere. It seemed as though the vault had simply decided to poke up through the earth. Now even geologists joined the investigation. Dr. Jack Renton of the West Virginia Geological Survey stated that he didn't know of any geological cause that could have forced the grave to open. Because the top of the coffin was only about four feet below the surface, Renton added, "I would find it very difficult to believe that natural gas could concentrate itself in something that shallow."

The Morgantown area is honeycombed with mines because of the coal industry, Chapman notes, and some people theorized that perhaps the ground had simply collapsed due to this. "But experts in that field never found any evidence to show that was the case. In fact that particular part of town was really not mined at all. The mystery only got deeper and deeper," he says. As for disturbances in the earth itself, the West Virginia University seismograph indicated that no tremors had occurred in the area during that time. Richard W. Laird, a professor of petroleum engineering at West Virginia University, noted that any tremor that could possibly have caused the disruption would definitely have been felt and recorded by the sensitive instruments. In addition, if a fault beneath the surface had opened, Laird said, the vault would have settled deeper into the ground instead of rising to the point where it punctured the surface.

But when the casket was exhumed, explosions or tremors of *any* kind were ruled out entirely and for one simple reason: sitting on top of the rounded casket lid was a flower and the commemorative plate that said, "Our Darling." If the casket had been moved in any way, those objects would have slid off the top. They remained in place, indicating that whatever force was involved had affected only the vault and didn't disturb the casket at all.

After a while, all leads and ideas ran out. There was nothing left to do but put little Harry back into his resting place. The boy's mother was never told of the incident for fear it would affect her already failing health. The rest of Harry's surviving family simply wanted to put the whole incident behind them. For Chief Bennie Palmer and Officer Ralph Chapman, the grave of Harry Spitz has left an indelible impression on their memories.

"I've thought about this many times over the years. Even today I drive by that cemetery three or four times a week, and I still wonder about it, why it happened," says Palmer. "I couldn't begin to guess even now. It was all so very strange— I've never came across anything that odd before or after that. And I've seen a lot of pretty strange things in my time."

The incident has also bothered Chapman over the years. There was something about Harry, something about the little boy that won't leave Chapman even today as he wonders about the child's life and death.

"A strange occurrence like that grave eruption, so weird and completely unexplained, is the kind of thing that just sticks with you. We looked at everything, considered every possibility, did every test we could imagine, and came up with nothing," he says.

On July 12, 1975, in the bright sunshine and humid, mid-afternoon heat of a mountain summer, a small group gathered at Oak Grove Cemetery to watch as little Harry Spitz was again laid to rest, reinterred in a new, sealed vault. All the secrets of the incident were being taken to the grave. How or why the vault blew apart was never discovered, nor was an explanation for the body's preservation ever found. But the officers, and even some townsfolk, have a tendency to glance at Harry's grave whenever they pass by the cemetery. Just checking, of course, to make sure he's behaving himself.

Fire House

In a middle-class suburban Chicago neighborhood of attractive bilevel houses, one homesite stood out from the rest. The lovely beige brick house, which had been standing only 24 hours before, was now reduced to rubble, having been leveled by a bulldozer. A parade of dump trucks hauled the debris away to unknown landfills. The bulldozer's driver dipped his hand into a small container of water, and as he continued plowing through the wreckage, he tossed the water in all directions around the machine. Holy water, a witness said. The equipment operator was only trying to protect himself. The house was almost demolished, but that didn't mean he was safe.

Officer Mike Merlo of the Orland Park Police Department stood by and watched the destruction. Months before, he had vowed never to set foot in that house again. But now he'd returned to see it destroyed. Some people said ghosts and spirits were the reason for the many strange fires and other phenomena in the house; other more scientific types said natural gases and soil abnormalities were probably responsible. Merlo didn't know what to believe, but he felt pretty sure it wasn't minerals that caused the house to set fire to its contents over and over again. After what he had seen, Merlo was just glad the house was now demolished.

Once the debris was cleared, the foundation was completely removed. It left a gaping hole, which, right after a few soil tests were performed workers rushed to fill with clay. Then they could leave and never have to come back, never be fearful of that site again. At least that's what they hoped.

Merlo was among the first of many police officers and firefighters who had responded to calls of strange and terrifying fires at the residence beginning in March 1988. The Iverson* family reported that a mysterious mist had filled the house, a white haze that smelled strongly of sulfur. No cause was determined for the mist, and firefighters left, only to return later to extinguish burning draperies and furniture. An eerie fact about this fire: it didn't burn walls or the floor of the house. It ignited from flames shooting out of an electrical wall socket, blue flames outlined in red that roared from the outlet as if under pressure, a physical impossibility in an electrical conduit.

"That flame shot out of the socket like a torch, and it lasted about 30 seconds," Officer Mike Merlo recalls. "After I saw that, I wouldn't go back in the house. It's easy to talk about it now, but it was scary then."

Fire investigators were puzzled, and the Iversons' insurance company ordered the room where the fire occurred rewired.

The rewiring job was performed by Lindsey Eller, a part-time police officer who is also an electrician. While he had no idea how flames could leap from an outlet, he did the job and thought it would take care of the problem. But two more unexplained fires broke out afterward. He was then told to rewire the entire house. Eller replaced every outlet and switch, installed a new meter fitting, replaced light fixtures, and even ran new wires from the meter to Commonwealth Edison's transformers. But still the fires continued. Equally puzzling was the

The Fire House looked harmless—but looks were deceiving.
(PHOTO OBTAINED VIA THE ILLINOIS FREEDOM OF INFORMATION ACT)

fact that Eller never found any damaged wiring in any of the wall sockets that had emitted blue flames. He did find an odd, cream-colored powder which smelled like sulfur, but laboratory analysis never could identify the powder or its components.

Investigators also looked at the possibility that natural gas leaks caused the mists and fires. Arson Investigator Lieutenant Steve Smith and his partner, Lieutenant Terry Hyland, stayed in the house overnight several times to try to solve the puzzle of the mist. Though the gas company had checked the house for leaks, none were found.

"One night the room filled with a white haze, and I couldn't see my hand in front of my face," says Smith. "There was a strong sulfur smell, and my eyes were burning. I took a sample of the mist in a vacuum container, but analysis showed nothing unusual." The investigators also used fog machines to trace air currents between floors, but they found none. Finally, after spending so much time in the house, they even had their own blood analyzed to see if anything unusual turned up. Nothing did.

To all appearances, the Iversons' house had been a perfectly normal home in a perfectly normal suburb, and the family had lived there uneventfully for seven years. The sudden onset of the frightening fires now had neighbors' tongues wagging. It was ghosts, they said, or poltergeists or demons. Whatever it was, it had to be supernatural, they insisted. As rumors spread, the Iversons' house became a virtual tourist attraction. Crowds sat on the street and waited for something to happen; they parked on the Iversons' lawn and walked boldly up to the windows to peek inside. Psychics and ghostbusters arrived, as did priests who blessed the house, prayed for it, and tried to exorcise it. All of this hoopla put an incredible emotional strain on the Iverson family. They were somewhat relieved when fire investigators finally told them to move out of the house until a cause for the weird occurrences could be determined.

With the family gone, a consulting engineering firm came in to run sophisticated tests, bringing an army of chemists, geologists, engineers, scientists, and experts in explosives, who swarmed through the house searching for clues and testing everything imaginable. They figured there had to be a rational explanation for all this, and they were determined to find it. Samples of paint, drywall, carpeting, and wood were tested. Soil borings were taken to see whether anything in the ground beneath the house might explain the fires. Every square inch of the house was scanned with infrared monitoring equipment to locate any unusual hot spots.

"They found only one hot spot in that house with the infrared," says Eller, "and that turned out to be two pieces of insulation in the attic that were slightly overlapping each other. That's how sensitive the equipment was."

All of this high technology yielded no answers. Still, Lindsey Eller was not a superstitious man. From the start, he had approached the whole puzzle as just that—a puzzle to be solved, perhaps a challenge. Despite the continuous string of events that didn't add up, he refused to buy into the irrational beliefs held by many of the townsfolk. Then he was involved in an incident that made him reevaluate his thinking.

Eller had been standing by at the house in case fire investigators needed him. As he was chatting in the kitchen with his nephew and police officer Jerry Esposito, they were joined by the Iverson's teenage daughter, Iris*. Although the family moved out, her school bus still dropped her off at the house, and she had to wait for her parents to come by and pick her up. As they all talked, a smoke detector on the second floor suddenly began to wail. So did Iris. She screamed hysterically and ran wildly through the house. "She looked like she didn't know which way she was going," Eller says.

Esposito grabbed a fire extinguisher he'd brought with him, and the three men rushed upstairs to find Iris's bedroom filled with smoke. But incredibly, the wispy smoke was confined to the room and appeared to stop right at the open doorway. They cautiously entered the room and were stunned to see a sizable flame roaring out of the wall socket. The hot blue flame, at least an inch in diameter, gushed from the outlet like a blowtorch and blasted across the room where it ignited the bed. Esposito tried to use his fire extinguisher, but its water container—which he had just filled—was mysteriously empty.

Eller's nephew grabbed the bedcovers and ran off with them while Esposito took the mattress and Eller dragged out the box springs. Since the smoldering items wouldn't fit through the window, the men pulled them down the stairs and out the front door. Eller tossed the heavy box springs to the ground, where it instantly burst into flames so intensely hot that the metal springs collapsed on themselves.

"The whole thing burned up within a minute," Eller recalls. "Usually the fabrics burn and leave a skeleton of metal springs, but these springs went from eight inches in height to almost nothing. I have absolutely no explanation for it."

Police, firefighters, and the local fire marshall soon arrived, and the first thing they did was blame poor Iris for the fire. Unable to determine any origins for the many blazes, they believed someone had to be starting them and felt Iris was probably making a strong bid for attention. Some investigators pointed out that the fires and other phenomena never occurred unless Iris was present, but she vehemently denied any involvement. Eller believed the girl, and when a shouting match ensued, he joined in.

"How the hell could she have started it?" he yelled. "She never did go upstairs, and she stayed right beside me downstairs the whole time before it started! Besides, how could she possibly have made flames come out of a wall socket?"

Everyone's nerves were frayed. Eller and the firefighters went back into the house to examine the fire scene. The fire marshal, concluding the flames were electrical in nature, insisted that Eller remove the guilty electrical outlet. Eller shook his head, but took the socket apart anyway. There were no burn marks on it, nor were there any on the wiring or inside the box. The fire marshall insisted the socket was responsible until Eller reminded the man of an important fact.

"Just how stupid can you be?" he asked incredulously. "There isn't even any electricity to this house right now! I disconnected it myself!" Sure enough, the power cable to the house was rolled up outside by the street transformer. The smoke detectors had gone off because they had a safety battery backup.

Eventually, anything that could possibly catch fire was removed from the house—furniture, carpeting, draperies, personal effects—until the house was but an empty shell. Yet nothing stopped the horrifying flames, and no one came close to figuring out why they persisted. The Iverson family never returned. By October the insurance company could take no more. Not wishing to assume any further liability, the company ordered the house torn down, paid off the Iversons, and put an end to the whole creepy affair.

"I honestly don't know what happened at that house," says Lieutenant Steve Smith. "It defied everything. We spent a lot of time trying to figure out what happened, hundreds of hours, and we never did find out anything solid. It's still an open case."

Newspapers ran photos of the demolition with the words "haunted house" ever-present in the headlines and captions. In public, insurance company representatives laughed at the notion that spirits were somehow involved, insisting it was some type of gas problem all along that simply couldn't be detected.

But on the day the house was reduced to rubble, folks still came to pray, and they still sprinkled holy water on the site.

The Creature of Whitehall

Washington County, New York, nestled along the eastern foothills of the Adirondack Mountains, is a woodland paradise. Its secluded forests are perfect for camping, hunting, and fishing, and local residents have always believed that no wild beast in those forests could ever present a serious danger to them. But that belief was briefly challenged in the late summer of 1976.

Tuesday, August 24, 1976

Marty Paddock and Paul Gosselin finished packing their pickup truck for a camping excursion late in the day. They favored the rugged isolation of a woodsy area near some misty and desolate swamps just outside the town of Whitehall. Driving along the winding mountain roads, they suddenly heard a blood-curdling screech echo through the dense forest. It sounded like a woman screaming horribly in distress. Paddock quickly stopped the truck, and the pair looked in the direction of the scream, listening for more sounds. But everything was silent.

After a few minutes, they drove a short distance farther down the road, then turned around and came back to park at the same spot. Night had fallen, and as they watched the darkness and waited, Paul Gosselin was startled by the movement of an immense shadowy figure along a barbed wire fence lining the roadway. The peculiar shape was at least seven or eight feet tall, and suddenly it began moving slowly toward the truck.

"Marty, get the hell out of here!" Gosselin shouted. Paddock hit the gas pedal, his truck fishtailing down the road, leaving nearly 50 feet of rubber in its wake.

The two friends went straight to the Whitehall police station to report what they'd seen, but police didn't believe their story of a giant beastlike thing on two legs coming at them from the woods. Paddock and Gosselin were determined to prove themselves, so they talked a friend into returning to the site with them. Feeling more than a bit edgy, the trio waited in the truck only a short time before they spotted the creature again in the distance. Now all three went back to the police station, insisting that officers go and take a look.

This was not the first time locals had reported seeing something like that in the woods—tales of a Sasquatch-like creature had been around for a long time. But this night, Officer Brian Gosselin was on duty, and because his own brother was among the trio making the report, he considered that the group must have seen *something* unusual. Being a nonbeliever in such bizarre beasts, however, he felt that what the three men saw was more likely a hoax being perpetrated against them.

"I followed through on their report, though, and contacted the sheriff's office because the location was technically out of the town's jurisdiction," says Gosselin, now retired. "They sent a deputy, along with some New York State police and a couple of our men. I didn't go that night."

Nearly a dozen police officers arrived at the scene, using powerful flashlights to pierce the darkness. Suddenly a sheriff's deputy yelled, "What the hell was that!?" In the distance, a creature lumbered through thick trees and brush, a hairy beast walking upright and estimated to be between seven and eight feet tall, far larger than any indigenous bear could be. It quickly disappeared into the night, and officers found footprints much wider and three times as long as a man's. One of the officers present was Sergeant Wilfred Gosselin, Brian and Paul's father, who concluded that, based on his own sighting and the descriptions given by the many eyewitnesses, something unusual had been sighted.

"I'm not saying this is a monster or anything else, but there is something out there, and it's no animal that belongs in the northern part of this state," he said.

Wednesday, August 25

Brian Gosselin was scheduled to work the midnight shift, but several hours before that he decided to go to the woods to try and see for himself the strange creature that his father and brother had spotted. He asked his colleague George Fox*, a state trooper, to accompany him to the location. Fox was on duty and drove up in his patrol car to meet Gosselin at the site. After studying their surroundings, they decided to split up in order to scan more of the area. The plan was to sit quietly in the dark—lights out, car engines off—and just wait for something to happen. A strip of woods about 100 yards wide ran down a slope, separating two open meadows. Gosselin parked in grass four feet high in the lower meadow, where the creature had been seen, and Fox sat in the upper meadow, keeping in contact with Gosselin by CB radio. Sitting patiently in the warm, late summer night, all they could hear were night birds, the gentle rustle of leaves as a small animal scurried about, and an occasional burst of static from the CB radio.

Time passed uneventfully. Finally, Gosselin got out of his car to look around and stretch his legs. Suddenly he heard the sound of something walking heavily through the woods between the two meadows. Almost immediately his CB radio crackled, and Fox's hushed voice said urgently, "Brian, I hear something! I hear something!"

Whatever was coming through the trees and brush was definitely weighty. Gosselin heard a whooshing noise as the thing he couldn't yet see moved rapidly through the tall grass toward

Brian Gosselin reenacted his encounter with a Sasquatch creature in August 1976. (Courtesy of Bill Brann)

him. Stepping back into the car, he fumbled in the dark for his .357 service Magnum and a 200,000 candlepower spotlight. Finding both, he crouched behind the open door, flipped on the spotlight, and sent a wash of bright light over the area. There, about 50 feet in front of his car, he saw the huge creature moving toward him. Gosselin froze in place.

The thing was easily more than seven feet in height, weighed at least 300 pounds, and was covered with long, scraggly hair that was thicker in some places than in others. It was slouched, its long, dangling arms reaching below its knees. But what caught Gosselin's attention immediately were the creature's eyes—huge, bulging eyes the diameter of soup cans glared right at him, and they were a bright fiery red.

"That was no bear, and it definitely wasn't a man in a monkey suit," Gosselin says. "It was built like a man to some extent, but it carried itself like an ape. I really don't know what it was."

The creature walked with great strides toward the car until the glaring spotlight surprised it. Stopping in its tracks, it threw its hands—not paws—up over its eyes and let out a deafening scream. Gosselin pulled the hammer back on his .357, and at the same time was aware of Fox's patrol car flying out of the upper meadow toward town, his voice shouting over the CB radio, "There's something here! There's something here!" The creature's screech would have made anybody's hair stand up on end, Gosselin says, "And mine sure did. It covered its eyes as though the light was hurting them, but the amazing thing was, it didn't look like it wanted to harm me. It

Artist's sketch of a creature similar to the one Brian Gosselin encountered (COURTESY OF BILL BRANN)

was just scared to hell as soon as I turned on the light. I could have shot it right in the head, neck, or chest area, but I didn't. I couldn't."

In that instant, Gosselin found himself feeling almost as though he was invading the creature's privacy. Gosselin readily admits that he was scared, but the beast stopped coming toward him and showed no signs of aggression. Then it turned abruptly and walked swiftly away, up through the trees toward where Fox had been parked. Gosselin kept the spotlight on it and could see its backbone clearly defined. Its buttocks were covered in mud and matted hair, as though it had recently sat in moist dirt. With each long stride it swung its arms in wide arcs. Then it was gone, and the woods fell silent once again.

Gosselin slumped into the front seat of his car and sat there alone for quite some time. There was something about those eyes and the creature's pained scream that had prevented him from pulling the trigger. Yes, he could have shot and killed it quite easily. "If I had," he says thoughtfully, "I would have either been a real rotten person, or I'd have been a hero in a certain sense. What if that was one of only a handful of those creatures left on earth? On the other hand, I could have pointed to it and said, 'There's the proof, lying right there.'"

Gosselin didn't blame the trooper for running off. Anyone who could face the imposing creature and claim no fear would certainly be lying, he thought. When he could no longer sit alone in the woods, he returned to town to begin working the midnight shift.

Thursday, August 26

Overnight, word of the encounter spread. Gosselin clocked off his shift at 8:00 A.M. and went home to find a gaggle of reporters camped out on his doorstep. He didn't want to talk to them. He just wanted to sleep after his exhausting experience. Some reporters understood, but the more annoying ones kept pressing him for a statement. Gosselin refused to talk and finally shooed everyone away. Later that day he decided to return to the scene in daylight for another look around.

Parking his car in the same spot he'd been the night before, he got out and searched the ground. There, compressed deeply in the mud, were huge footprints made by the creature. Gosselin placed his foot beside one of the impressions for a reference. It was quite impressive, several times larger than his in both length and width. The prints did not show any claw marks and were pressed so deeply into the ground that they must have been made by a creature of tremendous weight. The stride between footprints was huge, much longer than a man could make, especially a man trying to pretend he was a beast. This added to Gosselin's conviction that what he'd seen was indeed a very real but unknown creature.

The newspapers that evening were rather unkind to Gosselin. He was stunned to see himself quoted in words he'd never said. That night, he received a lot of heckling from townspeople and fellow officers alike. "People would walk up and ask me if I'd gotten my marbles back yet," he recalls. Miffed, he began denying everything, a strategy some in the press used to further fuel the fire by reporting that the whole incident was actually a hoax. Other officers who'd seen the creature were told by superiors to keep their experiences to themselves.

"The ones of us who said we saw something, we were made more or less the laughingstock for a while. You have no idea what it's like until you put those shoes on your feet. I shunned everyone," Gosselin says.

Friday, August 27

Reports of something crossing back and forth along the Poultney River from the New York side to the Vermont side brought a New York State Police trooper and a small group of people to the river's banks near Whitehall. There they found three gigantic footprints, one of them castable, each of them 19 inches long with a four-inch heel. The castable print, partially concealed beneath some brush, was slightly water damaged from rain the night before. Water had dripped steadily from the brush into the footprint, and those water impressions are also in the cast. It was sent to a police agency in Albany for examination. Brian Gosselin read the reports and listened to the stories with interest, but said nothing.

Despite numerous sightings in the next few weeks, Gosselin kept silent about the creature and continued to do so for the next 20 years. The footprint cast was returned to the state trooper, along with a report saying it could not be identified. No photographs were taken of the three footprints in sequence to document the stride length, though eyewitnesses said it was extremely long. But the possibility of a hoax in that particular instance was never ruled out.

Gosselin felt some vindication. "White is white and black is black, but when a footprint like that one is scientifically examined and the professionals can't prove what made it or where it came from, that's a shade of gray," he says. "It's an unknown. It tells me something was there, and I confess now that I'm glad I saw the creature."

The nonbeliever became a believer in life-forms other than those we know about. He asserts that just because we've yet to capture one does not mean they're not out there.

AFTERWORD

AT THIS WRITING, it's been over a year since I began *Hidden Files*. I still keep in touch with many of the police officers I've met. It seems we just can't stop discussing the phenomena they've experienced. We still dissect the events, come up with theories, and imagine the possibilities. We wonder when there will be solid explanations for the unexplainable. We are continuously questioning—and this is how it should be.

I tell them about some stories that "got away," a few, which for various reasons, I could not examine in this book: an officer who encountered a lake monster in northern California, a haunted U.S. Navy carrier, a rock-throwing poltergeist, and more. We always have plenty to talk about. But do we come to any conclusions?

Yes—that a lot of people have had very strange but real experiences, and that sometimes they have had problems overcoming the stigma often attached to those experiences. Many of the officers admit that they feel better for having told their stories. For most, with a few exceptions, life went on as usual after their encounters. Some are still unable to cope fully with what happened to them. But we all hope that the unsolved cases will finally be solved—that perpetrators will be brought to justice, that the whereabouts of the missing will be discovered.

Personally, I acknowledge that the skepticism I felt about some subjects is now gone. I'm absolutely convinced of the existence of certain phenomena, while before I was not. Along with the anecdotes, I have presented what I believe is rational and thought-provoking information on the various subjects, information that has helped me to arrive at my own conclusions. I agree with the assertion that a closed mind can close out the truth. I also believe that only through open-minded examination and serious research will we move toward scientific explanations for that which we now call paranormal. Once we have *all* the facts, we will all get to the truth.

THE POLICE OFFICERS

Lieutenant Jim Duff *("U'hane")*

Jim Duff joined the Honolulu Police Department on April 1, 1971, as a patrol officer. During his 27 years with the department, Duff was promoted to sergeant, detective, and then lieutenant. He received many commendations for his work, both from his superiors and from the citizens of Honolulu. He prides himself most on his work with cases involving the average citizen and on his work with domestic violence cases.

"Getting the women to go through with prosecuting such cases was an accomplishment," Duff says. "I would put a lot of effort into investigating the cases and making them airtight by locking witnesses into their testimony. This way, if the victims changed their minds six months later and didn't want to prosecute their attackers, they couldn't go up on the witness stand and change their stories. To me, this is what I was getting paid for." The result was that in many of the severe cases, the offenders were put away for attempted murder rather than simple assault.

Duff enjoyed being a cop off duty as well. He often worked as a film extra, portraying Honolulu police officers on several television shows filmed in the islands. He can be seen in more than 30 episodes of "Magnum PI," several episodes of "Hawaii Five-O," and even had speaking parts in "Jake and the Fatman." Duff also did stunt driving on "Hawaii Five-O." He retired from the force as a lieutenant in April 1996 and now resides in Austin, Texas.

Ed Hill ("The Shaman of Teslin Lake")

Staff Sergeant Ed Hill joined the Royal Canadian Mounted Police (RCMP) in Toronto on July 29, 1968. He trained in Saskatchewan and was first posted to Surrey, British Columbia, in January 1969. Over many years, serving in many Canadian towns, Hill worked both as a uniformed constable and in undercover work. He is now a detachment commander in the town of Hope, British Columbia. The highlight of his career, says Hill, has been his work with native peoples, who have embraced him as one of their own.

"I am particularly proud of the names given to me by native families who have 'adopted' me," he says. "I have two names—*Anisnass*, which means 'guardian of the spirit,' and *Klakleeleekla*, which means 'If you come to my home I will feed you.' I take this very seriously and use the names only in appropriate circumstances."

Hill was awarded the RCMP's Long Service Medal and the Canada 125 Medal, given on Canada's 125th anniversary to law enforcement officers and citizens in recognition for their work within and for a community.

Rich Strasser ("The Spirit of Motherhood")

After graduating from the University of Idaho and owning a business for several years, Rich Strasser decided to become a law enforcement officer and joined the El Dorado County Sheriff's Office in 1992. As a patrol officer, he has worked on cases ranging from burglaries to narcotics. His most important case was also his department's most recognized one—the Skubish disappearance. He was awarded his department's Medal of Valor for saving Nicky Skubish's life. Strasser is now a member of the Special Weapons and Tactics (SWAT) team and also trains new recruits.

Jim Riffle ("The Barracks")

Jim Riffle became a West Virginia State Trooper in 1976 and was stationed at the barracks in Berkeley Springs for 11 years. He is currently a first sergeant and district commander, supervising several state police detachments in several West Virginia counties. Though he spent a good part of his career as a road trooper, Riffle prefers criminal investigation work such as domestic disputes, lost children, and homicides. "Our duties entail every type of situation possible," he says. "It's appealing to me because it's always something different every day."

Tim Moss ("Heavy Psi")

Lieutenant Tim Moss has been with the LAPD for 26 years. He started as a patrol officer and has moved through many divisions and ranks, including the court liaison unit, juvenile division, training, homicide, and internal affairs. While working the streets, Moss made over 1,000 narcotics arrests in a three-year period and as a homicide detective worked over 100 murder cases. He was detective coordinator for four LAPD divisions before being promoted to his current position as watch commander of the West Valley Division. Moss has received more than 80 commendations for his work.

Robert Lee ("The Detective and the Psychic")

Robert Lee began his law enforcement career in January 1971 in Reno, Nevada. After three and a half years (and being shot in the line of duty), he left police work for a while because, he says, "I became disillusioned with the court system." But he was hooked on the work. Four years later, he joined the Lincoln City Police Department in Oregon, where he served as a detective for nearly three years. He then moved on to his current department in Lake Oswego, where he's been for 15 years. Though he has worked on his share of murder and narcotics cases, Lee's specialty is white-collar and computer crime. He admits to being pretty good at removing information from a computer hard drive.

"I prefer the medium-hard to hard cases over the simple ones," he says. "Anything with numbers attached: frauds, embezzlements, thefts. One of my favorite cases involved a guy who embezzled more than $343,000 dollars from his employer over a period of 11 months. The employer didn't know about it until the crook was fired for some other reason. His replacement discovered the guy had been stealing money in every direction. I caught the guy, and I thought it was a fun case because there were so many different aspects to it."

After 11 years in the Lake Oswego Police Department's Detective Division, Lee decided to go back in uniform and return to patrol work. He also serves as a field training officer and works with new recruits.

Greg Adair ("Ancient Medicine")

Greg Adair graduated from the Window Rock Navajo Police Academy in October 1978 and joined the Navajo Police Department (NPD) as an officer in the juvenile division. He became an investigator and was promoted to sergeant and supervisor of criminal investigation. He was named Criminal Investigator of the Year in 1983. Later he moved to patrol work as a patrol sergeant. In 1986, he left the NPD for a temporary job with the Mojave County Sheriff's Office while his wife attended college in Tucson. He then moved to Colorado City, Arizona, for a year to help start up the new police department. Adair returned to the Navajo Police Department in 1992, where he now works as a criminal investigator. He has received commendations for his work, including a letter from the U.S. Attorney's Office for his work on a homicide case.

Ron Chancey ("Encounter")

Ron Chancey became a Florida state trooper in 1970 and remained with the force for eight years. He then moved to the Hillsborough County Sheriff's Office in Tampa. There he received numerous commendations for his work in investigations, including the arrest of Billy Ferry, who firebombed a supermarket and killed five people. In 1989 he moved to the Dade City Police Department as a patrol officer and detective, and in 1993 joined the Hernando County Sheriff's Office. Chancey attended the University of North Florida Traffic Institute and the Florida Highway Patrol Academy and studied criminal justice at Hillsborough Community College and Pasco-Hernando Community College. A large part of Chancey's career involved murder cases and traffic accident investigations—situations where he had to deal with the families of victims. He says he learned the most about handling victims after becoming the victim of a violent crime himself.

"As a law enforcement officer, you do your darnedest to comfort victims of crime, but all the education you get in the academies might not be enough," he says. "When I became the victim of a violent crime, it changed my outlook and made me look back on it all. I could see where I could have done better, and I learned to be more responsive to victims."

Chancey is now retired and living in north Florida.

Josiah Lemon ("Invasion of the Corn Stompers")

Josiah "Joe" Lemon became sheriff of rural Mercer County, Illinois, in November 1966, after serving for many years as the county road commissioner. He and his wife lived at the county jail, where he cared for prisoners in addition to his duties as the area's top law enforcement officer. This included policing many small towns that did not have their own police departments. During his career, Sheriff Lemon handled all manner of cases, including murders, bank robberies, drownings, accidents, and burglaries. He is now retired and still lives in Mercer County.

Kenny Graham ("Chase")

In June 1996, Kenny Graham was promoted to sergeant and returned to the patrol division where he first started his career with the Jefferson County Police Department in 1982. Over the years, Graham has worked as a burglary detective, a patrol officer, and a helicopter patrolman/pilot. He has received numerous commendations for his work.

"I really loved flying choppers and the work that involved," Graham says. "I remember finding and rescuing an elderly Alzheimer's patient one cold winter night by using infrared equipment. Helping people is what it's all about."

Though he no longer flies choppers on duty, Graham still serves as a flight instructor for the department.

Greg Laumbach ("An Incident in Mora County")

Deputy Greg Laumbach began his career with two New Mexico agencies, working part time as a livestock inspector for the New Mexico State Livestock Board and part time as a deputy with the Mora County Sheriff's Office. In the summer of 1996, he hired on full time as a deputy with the Livestock Board and continues to work livestock cases. He reports that he has not seen a case of unexplained mutilation since the story he related for this book.

Rick Chapman (*"Obatala"*)

Rick Chapman always wanted to be a Beaufort County sheriff's deputy and got his wish in 1973. He worked the county jail and dispatch for two years until a road patrol position came open. Since then he has received numerous awards and commendations for his work, including one for capturing an armed robber and another for preventing a young girl from committing suicide with a gun. Chapman has been involved in every aspect of the sheriff's office work during his career. He began the department's first driving course, was second in command for implementing a Special Weapons and Tactics (SWAT) team, and served on the Hostage Negotiation Team for four years. Chapman attended the South Carolina Criminal Justice Academy and is a 1995 graduate of the prestigious FBI National Academy in Quantico, Virginia.

Sharon Lansdowne ("Diary of a Mad Housewife")

Sharon Lansdowne entered uncharted waters when she joined the San Jose Police Department on March 1, 1966. At that time, women were not hired as patrol or police officers, and she was one of two women hired as identification officers. The job involved record maintenance and performing reference checks for officers in the field. But Lansdowne soon went on to become the first woman sent to the San Jose Police Academy, graduating as a full patrol officer.

"I wore this cute little uniform with a skirt and high heels that looked more like a flight attendant's uniform," she recalls with a laugh. "The purse that went with the uniform had a flap that covered my gun, mace, and handcuffs, but if I needed any of those things, I had to throw my wallet out to get to them." But women on the force eventually showed that a police officer didn't have to walk and talk tough to do the job, she says. "We did the job in a different way, and we had to go through a lot to prove ourselves, but I wouldn't have traded the experience for a minute."

Lansdowne worked patrol for eight years and became the department's first female training officer. Her subsequent assignments included the juvenile unit, narcotics, and missing persons, where she worked on the Caroline Rubia case. She performed lots of undercover work, and once set herself up as a decoy for a serial rapist, pretending to be a prostitute in a case that eventually became a murder investigation. She has received numerous commendations for her work, including the Rubia case.

Lansdowne retired in January 1995. Her husband is chief of police in Richmond, California.

Ray Jarvis ("Idaho Gothic")

In the late 1950s, Ray Jarvis had his first taste of law enforcement work while stationed with the army at Fort Sill, Oklahoma. After his military stint with the army police, Jarvis returned to Idaho and farmed for three years before becoming the village marshal in the town of Paul. That began his 31-year career. "That's when I decided that law enforcement was what I wanted to do with the rest of my life," he says.

In 1963, Jarvis became a deputy with the Minidoka County Sheriff's Office, where he was promoted to chief deputy and then elected sheriff in 1976. He attended the National Sheriff's Academy in Los Angeles and served four terms before his election defeat in 1992. A large part of his career involved drug enforcement. "The remoteness of the area and its location along a major route from the southern U.S. border to Seattle made Minidoka County attractive to drug traffickers. We've made a lot of big drug busts over the years," Jarvis says. He is now retired and lives in Rupert.

Tom Bennett ("Missing: Philip Taylor Kramer")

Tom Bennett joined the Ventura County Sheriff's Office in October 1980. His career has run the gamut from street patrol and custody patrol to administration and investigation. Deputy Bennett was named Officer of the Year a few years ago and has received commendations from the FBI for apprehension of bank robbery suspects. He considers his specialties to be cases involving stolen vehicles and other property crimes.

France Michaud ("Missing: David Churchill Jackson")

France Michaud joined the Pembroke Pines Police Department in Florida in November 1983 as a road patrol officer. But she had a special interest in crimes against children and families, so she pursued the special training necessary to investigate these types of crimes. In August 1987, she became a detective for the department, assigned to work on cases involving missing persons, child abuse, and sex crimes. She has received numerous departmental and civilian commendations for her work.

"The challenge of this type of work comes in dealing with the victims, especially children. It can be very difficult to get children to bond with you and trust you," says Detective Michaud. "It's almost like being a psychologist, social worker, and police officer all at once. But I love the work and believe that if I can help one person, I'm really accomplishing something."

Douglas Glamann ("Other Phenomena")

Chief Douglas Glamann began his career with the Dodge County Sheriff's Office in Iron Ridge, Wisconsin. He moved to the Horicon Police Department where he worked the night shift for eight years. He was promoted to chief of police directly from the night shift in 1987. Within six months the town's famous poltergeist case broke open. Glamann is a graduate of the FBI's Law Enforcement Executive Development Program and works closely with state and federal law enforcement agencies in his area.

Wilbur Williams ("Katherine")

Wilbur Williams was studying for a degree in Criminal Justice at the University of South Alabama when he decided to join the Mobile Police Department "just to get some more experience in the field." That was in 1973, and he's been with the department ever since. Williams was promoted to sergeant in 1978, worked a stint at the city jail, then transferred to the Criminal Investigations Division as a homicide detective. He was promoted to lieutenant in 1986 and moved to the Criminal Intelligence Division, where he kept tabs on known and suspected criminals. "It was snooping, basically—spy-type stuff," he explains. "We worked as clandestine, undercover operatives as part of a federal program that applied tricks of the intelligence community to domestic law enforcement."

Williams went on to obtain a master's degree in Criminal Justice Administration from Troy State University. In 1989, he was selected to attend the FBI National Academy where he was honored as session spokesman for his class, the 156th session. While attending the academy, he was again promoted, this time to the rank of captain, in a ceremony held at the academy in Quantico, Virginia. A year later, Williams was promoted to major and returned to the investigative division as chief of detectives. He moved to Support Services in 1996, his current position.

Williams has received several departmental commendations for his work over the years. He plans to run for sheriff of Mobile County when he "retires" in 1998.

Bennie Palmer ("The Grave of Harry Spitz")

After serving in the Korean War, Bennie Palmer joined the Monogalia County, West Virginia, police force in July 1954. He then moved to the Morgantown Police Department on New Year's Day, 1957, and stayed for the rest of his career. Palmer was promoted to lieutenant in 1965 and was in charge of the force's new investigative department. Three years later he was promoted to chief of police, a job he held for 12 years. A change in city management at that time led him to ask for a return to a lieutenant's position, where he was placed in charge of officer training until his retirement in 1985.

Palmer's numerous honors include Police Officer of the Year. While he was chief, he received the FBI's J. Edgar Hoover

Award for promoting a well-trained department and operating according to FBI standards. He was appointed by West Virginia's then-governor Jay Rockefeller to the Governor's Committee on Crime, Delinquency, and Corrections where he served for eight years. He continued to work in that area after retirement, serving on the state's Department of Corrections Committee on Regional Jails.

Lindsey Eller ("Fire House")

Lindsey Eller has been in law enforcement for 12 years. After attending the Blue Island Police Academy in Illinois, he has worked for two suburban Chicago police departments. He is currently a part-time sergeant assigned to the patrol division with the Calumet City Police Department. He has received several commendations for solving burglary investigations, including one that solved 33 separate cases.

Steve Smith ("Fire House")

Steve Smith has worked in fire service for over 19 years as a paramedic and firefighter, and for the past 10 years as an arson investigator. He has spent his entire career with Orland Park Fire District and has received several commendations for his work as a paramedic.

Brian Gosselin ("The Creature of Whitehall")

Brian Gosselin comes from a family of law enforcement officers and became a patrol officer himself in 1975 when he joined the Whitehall Police Department. In 1986, he moved to the Granville Police Department in New York as a patrolman. But in 1989 Gosselin was forced to retire after an on-duty automobile accident during a high-speed chase left him permanently disabled. During his career, Gosselin received letters of commendation from the New York State Police for his outstanding work, which ranged from capturing escaped federal convicts to recovering many stolen vehicles.